Venice

Jack Altman and
Barbara Ender-Jones

GW00691789

JPMGUIDES

Divided into six *sestieri* (districts), Venice is a mosaic of islands separated by some 180 canals and linked by more than 400 bridges. It's a delight to stroll through this magical city, where more than nine buildings out of ten are historic monuments.

Contents

Features

Shopping in
San Marco 26
Grand Canal Cruise 30
Painting 46
Venice for Children 56
Risi e Bisi 83
Cinema's Love Affair 88

Maps

San Marco 99
Lido, La Giudecca 100
Murano, Burano 102

Fold-out maps

Venice
Venice, the islands
and the lagoon
Vaporetti lines

cityLights 5
cityPast 11
citySights 19
    San Marco 20
    Dorsoduro 34
    Santa Croce 42
    San Polo 50
    Cannaregio 58
    Castello 64
    The Islands 70
cityBites 77
cityNights 84
cityFacts 91
Index 103

Our favourite sights are
marked with a star ★
in the table at the
beginning of each
section.

cityLights

I'm So Gorgeous

Never was vanity more justified. This is not a town that waited for others to pay it compliments. Like a gorgeous film star, Venice has always known it is beautiful. It called itself La Serenissima and bestowed upon itself the title of "Queen of the Adriatic", ceremonially sealed with an annual wedding between its ruler, the Doge, and the sea – a pageant which is re-enacted today for the benefit of modern visitors. The Venetians didn't wait for travel brochures. In 1581, Francesco Sansovino, son of the town's great Renaissance architect, put forward the theory in his history of Venice that the name Venetia derived from the Latin *Veni Etiam*: "Come again and again – for however oft you come, you will always see new things and new beauties." Linguistically, he was wrong; the name's etymology remains a mystery to this day. But the rest of the statement is perfectly true. With its 177 canals and 450 bridges, its scores of *palazzi*, whether glorious or dilapidated, this magical city on the lagoon remains an inexhaustible source of discoveries. Seek out secluded corners, and create your own personal Venice.

Undeniably Grand Canal

The introduction to the city is astonishing. The very first boat ride along the Grand Canal opens up vistas that cannot be compared with anywhere else on earth. You coast by 200 palaces and churches that have been built over a period of 600 years. Some people like to point out the many different architectural styles, ranging from Venetian-Byzantine to the most decorative Flamboyant Gothic and august Renaissance, ornate baroque and the last defiant outpouring of neoclassical. Others are content to imagine themselves among the countesses and merchant princes, rascally diplomats and opera singers who once called these *palazzi* their homes.

The S-shaped Canale Grande winds for more than 4 km (2.5 miles) through a city built up on pinewood stilts driven 8 m (26 ft) into a seabed of silt and clay. The lagoon numbers in all 118 islets, home to just 80,000 permanent residents. In the town's heyday, the population numbered 200,000. After years of recurrent floods and subsidence, fears that Venice would sink completely beneath the waves are being countered by the heroic efforts of UNESCO-sponsored engineers, geologists and art historians. So drop off your bags and start out on your first exploration.

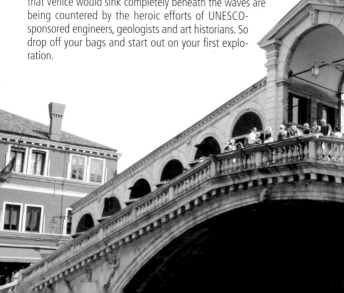

Get Lost

Like the countless pigeons, the vast majority of visitors stick to Piazza San Marco, never daring to wander far from this great square leading out to the Grand Canal. With its great basilica, the soaring Campanile, the Doge's Palace and its Bridge of Sighs, not forgetting the museum in the Palazzo Correr telling the story of the city's 1,300 glorious years, the square certainly has sufficient beauty, grandeur and history to absorb all their attention, while ready relief from sightseeing is provided by the enthralling bustle in the arcades of shops and cafés.

But there is so much more. Away from the great squares and formidable *palazzi*, all the back streets and canals are waiting to be explored. People are wrongly afraid of losing their way – all over the place, there are yellow street signs pointing you back to the safety of Piazza San Marco. Nevertheless, getting lost in this most bewitching of towns is one of the best things that could happen to you. No cars! Silence. Stand on a hump-

Pause a while to watch the river traffic from the Rialto bridge.

backed bridge of brick or limestone and watch a delivery-man rowing his boatful of milk-crates or vegetables to an outlying customer, or a couple of young – or not so young – lovers gliding by in a gondola. Or sit in a little piazza behind the railway station, among the modest houses of the old Jewish Ghetto and feed the few pigeons who, like you, have escaped the crowd.

Beyond the Piazza

As a first venture away from Piazza San Marco, cross the bridge to the Galleria dell'Accademia and spend a couple of hours in the company of splendid paintings by Giorgione, Bellini, Carpaccio, Titian and Veronese. Or wander over to find out what's new on the Rialto, the great bridge where the merchants of Venice have always exacted, if not a pound of flesh, the best price for jewellery, perfumes, shoes, clothes and trinkets.

Beyond the Accademia, you can walk over to the Zattere and watch the big ocean-going vessels push aside the *vaporetti* (water buses) and little *motoscafi* (water taxis). On the point of the lagoon, the wonderful domed baroque church of Santa Maria della Salute awaits your visit: for too many people it remains just a romantic landmark on the skyline. In fact it contains a superb Tintoretto and other fine paintings by Titian.

In the other direction is Veronese's delightful church of San Sebastiano, his burial place and veritable museum for some of his finest work. If your taste happens to be more modern, right near to the Accademia is the Palazzo Venier dei Leoni housing the magnificent collection of 20th-century art of the Peggy Guggenheim Foundation.

The artistic choice is endless: Titian's great altarpiece in the Frari church, the monumental

series of paintings by Tintoretto in the venerable guild of Scuola di San Rocco, the series by Carpaccio in the guild of the Schiavoni (Dalmatians).

And So Much More

Take time, too, for a closer look at the façades of palaces which the Venetians, with characteristic false modesty, often preferred to call houses (Ca'): the exquisite Gothic Ca' d'Oro and Ca' Foscari, or the superb baroque Ca' Rezzonico. Children love the grotesque masks on Palazzo Pesaro.

Of the islands out in the estuary, Murano is famous for its glassware, Burano for its lace and Torcello for its beautiful cathedral. The Lido has the old-fashioned elegance of a classical seaside resort, a fine sandy beach, a casino and luxury hotels. Rent a bicycle and explore it from one end to the other.

For many, Venice is a non-stop festival – Mardi Gras carnival with fantastic costumes and masks, the formidable summer Biennale, avant-garde festivals of fine arts, music and theatre, and in September, the film festival. Venice's churches provide a magnificent setting for concerts, notably the organ recitals at St Mark's. Opera at La Fenice has always counted among the finest in Europe, and when fire destroyed the interior of the theatre in 1996, no time was wasted in finding an alternative during reconstruction. Performances carried on regardless in a tent set up on Tronchetto and in the historic Teatro Malibran near the Rialto. Mozart's *Don Giovanni*, the opera that epitomizes the Venetian spirit, is known as a *dramma gioccoso*, a playful drama. That's Venice.

FAMOUS FOOTSTEPS

Robert Browning

(1812–89)
The English poet was such a fixture in Venetian life that his home in the famous Ca' Rezzonico became known in his last years as Palazzo Browning. A plaque there quotes his own epitaph:
Open my heart and you will see,
graved inside of it "Italy".

Ca' Rezzonico

cityPast

Reluctant Beginnings

They didn't really want to go there, but the barbarians left them no choice. In ancient times, the lagoon was just a place for coastal dwellers to go fishing around the little islands and extract salt for winter food-storage. Then, as the Roman Empire crumbled, successive waves of invaders drove them away from the Adriatic coast to seek shelter in the offshore archipelago. First came the Goths in 402, then Attila and his Huns 50 years later. As soon as the dust of pillage had settled, many of the refugees moved their homes back to the mainland. But increasingly, as the raids grew more frequent, people stayed behind to make more permanent communities out of their island settlements. In their flat-bottomed barges, the lagoon people prospered, already, by trading surplus goods around the waterways of central and northern Italy. After the invasion in 568 of the Lombards who, unlike the hit-and-run Goths and Huns, had clearly come to stay, the people of the lagoon formed a solid confederation of communities calling themselves collectively the Venetiae.

In 697, the Venetians chose a doge (local dialect for the Latin *dux*) to head their provincial government, initially answerable to the Byzantine emperor in Constantinople. Installed on Malamocco island out by the Lido, Orso was the first of an unbroken line of 118 doges that lasted 1,100 years. In 774, the Venetians withstood attack by an army of Franks led by Charlemagne's son, Pépin, but were forced to move their capital to Rivo Alto (Rialto), the island of the present Doge's Palace and Piazza San Marco. (Malamocca was engulfed by a tidal wave in 1107.)

Republic Rules the Waves

Venice's rise to power and riches in the Middle Ages was marked by masterful shipbuilding and brazen trading methods. Ignoring the strictures of Constantinople and Rome, the city traded with Muslims in lumber, salt and slaves. With Arab gold, the Venetians bought oriental silks and spices from Constantinople for resale in western Europe at huge profits. In times when merchants habitually moon-lighted as pirates, the fast and sturdy Venetian fleet gradu-

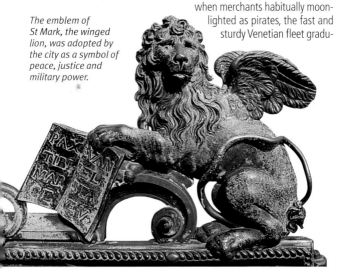

The emblem of St Mark, the winged lion, was adopted by the city as a symbol of peace, justice and military power.

ally won control of the Adriatic from their ruthless but undisciplined Dalmatian rivals. In 1000, Doge Pietro Orseolo II celebrated the Republic's domination by tossing a diamond ring into the water in a ritual "wedding to the sea", which became an annual tradition. Venice extended its maritime supremacy across the eastern Mediterranean and borrowed Levantine styles in the sumptuous architecture of the 11th-century basilica of San Marco, the city's patron saint.

From 1095, the Crusades proved a boon to the city's treasury. The Venetians became high-priced charter-travel agents and even higher-priced arms manufacturers for the mission to "save" the Holy Land. Never letting religion interfere with business, Venice required the European armies to earn their passage by knocking off the Republic's trade rivals on their way to Palestine. On the Fourth Crusade (1202–04), the French and Flemish soldiers never even got there. After a first stop-over to massacre Venice's enemies on the Croatian coast, the knights were shipped straight to Constantinople. With the promise of fabulous riches in this capital of the eastern Christian empire, the knights went on a ferocious rampage of plunder, rape and murder. By Doge Enrico Dandolo's prearranged plan to secure control of the eastern Mediterranean, Venice put its own man on the imperial throne – and obtained the lion's share of the booty to pay for the trip. The brutality of the stratagem won the hatred of eastern and western Christendom alike, but it carried the Republic to the zenith of its power and the merchants of Venice cried all the way to the bank.

Tough at the Top

In the late 13th century, adding prudence to audacity, the Venetians decided that their empire was too big for one man. The doge was reduced to a purely ceremonial role, a majestic bird in exotic plumage wandering around the gilded cage of his palace. The Great Council of 1,000 aristocrats entrusted governmental decisions to a Council of Ten.

In the Mediterranean, Venice had to fight it out with mighty Genoa for control of Cyprus, Crete and other Greek islands. They also competed for the Black Sea's lucrative markets in grain and slaves, or the spices-for-cloth trade in London, Bruges and Antwerp. It was Venetian and Genoese cargoes from the Crimea that brought plague-bearing rats and the Black

Death of 1348 to western Europe. Venice lost half its population in just over a year. But it was still able to muster enough courage and resources to throw back the last but most menacing of the Genoese attacks, right at the gateway to the lagoon in 1379.

The success tempted Venice to over-extend its power. In the 15th century, besides gobbling up more major ports around Greece and Albania, it moved onto the Italian mainland and provoked Milan, Naples and Florence into forming a hostile alliance. At sea, a more serious threat arose with the Turkish conquest of Constantinople in 1453, irrevocably weakened by the Venetian-led destruction 250 years earlier. The Republic lost a vital battle at Negroponte (modern Khalkis on the Aegean island of Euboea) in 1470 and gave up more key trading counters to the Ottoman Turks along the Adriatic and Aegean coasts over the next 30 years.

At the same time, the exploits of two great navigators knocked the commercial wind out of Venice's sails in the Mediterranean. In 1492, Christopher Columbus turned eyes to the riches of the Americas. Six years later, Portugal's Vasco da Gama ended Venice's virtual monopoly of the spice trade by opening up a new route to India around Africa's Cape of Good Hope.

The Golden Decline

Back home, the town's era of greatness was being immortalized by its artists and scholars. Just as the religiously devout were drawn to the Holy Places of Jerusalem, so profane pilgrims flocked to Venice to see the architecture of

◀ *The golden basilica was built as a shrine for St Mark's remains, stolen in Alexandria and brought to Venice in 828 by two merchants.*

Jacopo Sansovino and Andrea Palladio and the paintings of Giovanni Bellini, Giorgione, Carpaccio, Titian, Veronese and Tintoretto. They proved to be the Republic's most brilliant beacons before its power began to wane.

Throughout the 16th century, the popes and Emperor Charles V whittled away at Venice's holdings on mainland Italy. The Republic knew a brief moment of glory in 1571 when its fleet played a leading role in the Holy League's prestigious victory over the Turks at Lepanto, but at the same time it lost its strategic outpost of Cyprus. In ending the myth of Turkish invincibility, Venice was also relegated from the league of great powers.

The native talent Venice had previously devoted to conquering overseas markets was now given over to the gentler art of good living. The quality of its new textiles, glassware and book printing, and its time-honoured commercial know-how, ensured a less spectacular but still comfortable income. Having survived its turbulent centuries on the world stage without the ravages of foreign invasion, the town's palaces and churches remained splendidly intact. While any self-respecting gentleman's Grand Tour of 18th-century Europe would inevitably include the august cities of Rome, Athens and Florence, Venice was considered the most enjoyable of all, whether for the finesse of the operas and concerts of Monteverdi and Vivaldi and the theatre of Goldoni, or for the more outrageous pleasures of the Carnival. Never was a brothel more elegant than when set in a baroque palazzo on the Grand Canal.

Tears of Grief and Joy

Napoleon Bonaparte put a bitter end to the glittering Venetian adventure. His forces conquered all of Venice's territories on the mainland, and an ultimatum demanded total surrender. On May 12, 1797, exactly 11 centuries after the election of the first doge, the 118th and last, Lodovico Manin, tearfully abdicated as the Great Council voted to dissolve the Most Serene Republic. Carefully guided by French art experts, Bonaparte's troops plundered the treasures of the palaces and churches. Taken from the monastery of San Giorgio Maggiore, Veronese's monumental Wedding Feast of Cana, along with two other of his paintings from the Doge's Palace, still hang in the Louvre. As a supreme humiliation, the soldiers burned the Bucintoro, the grandiose galley from which the doge performed his wedding ceremony with the sea.

In the 19th century, Venice was ruled by the Austrian Habsburgs. They brought back many of the artistic treasures looted by the French and, for the first time, linked the city to the mainland by a railway built in 1846. Venetians joined the European wave of revolt of 1848 and drove out the Austrian troops, but independence was short-lived as the Habsburgs re-established their authority for another 17 years. In a plebiscite following the Prussian victory over Austria in 1866, the Venetians finally threw in their lot with the rest of Italy, voting to join the new kingdom.

Since then it has been content, more or less, to become a glorious backwater.

Keeping Afloat

Water has remained a major preoccupation as successive administrations and world experts sponsored by UNESCO fight to keep the city from sinking into the lagoon or being eaten away by pollution. The annual influx of 12 million tourists is a major problem, and authorities are perpetually threatening to impose a tax on visitors to help pay for cleaning up after them – or to limit their numbers.

Henry James set his *Portrait of a Lady* and *Wings of the Dove* in Venice, while Thomas Mann, of course, immortalized it in his novel *Death in Venice*. The international film festival on the Lido, the first such in the world, was the brainchild of Benito Mussolini – and one of the few lasting cultural benefits that Italy gained from his rule. An international playground – and workshop – for the rich and famous, the town welcomed Ernest Hemingway, who settled a while on the island of Torcello, and Peggy Guggenheim, who installed her great modern art collection in the Palazzo Venier dei Leoni.

But for the rest of us mere mortals, it is still the place where lovers come to mend a broken heart – or break a whole one.

citySights

San Marco 20
All roads and canals lead to the city centre

Dorsoduro 34
Peaceful residential district

Santa Croce 42
A wall of palaces along the Grand Canal

San Polo 50
Around the Rialto

Cannaregio 58
The working part of the city, and the old ghetto

Castello 64
Charm and atmosphere around the Arsenal

The Islands 70
Each with its own personality

SAN MARCO

This is the historic, political, cultural and architectural centre of the city. Here, within the southern loop of the Grand Canal, you find most of the historic monuments and churches, as well as many restaurants, shops, big hotels and banks.

THE DISTRICT AT A GLANCE

🏛 **SIGHTS**

Architecture
Basilica ★ 20
Campanile 21
Torre dell'Orologio ...23
Palazzo Ducale ★ 23
Ponte dei Sospiri ★ ...24
San Zulian 24
San Salvador 24
Ponte di Rialto ★ 24
La Fenice ★ 25

Scala Contarini del
Bóvolo 25
San Moisè 25
Santo Stefano ★ 25
Ponte
dell'Accademia 25

Art
Palazzo Grassi 25

Atmosphere
Piazza San Marco ★..24

Books
Biblioteca Marciana .23

Browsing
Mercatino
Antiquariato 25

Museums
Museo
Civico Correr 22
Museo
Archeologico 22

👫 **WALKING
TOUR   78**

☕ **WINING AND
DINING   28**

Piazza San Marco (E5) The religious and political centre of Venice, Saint Mark's Square – the only piazza in Venice – is lined on three sides by splendid palaces. To the north are the Procuratie Vecchie, dating from the 12th century, originally the headquarters of the city's "procurator" (high magistrate, second only to the Doge) and nowadays used as offices. To the south are the Procuratie Nuove, and on the east side the Ala Napoleonica housing the Museo Correr.

Basilica di San Marco (F5) When two merchants brought the remains of St Mark to Venice from Alexandria, he was declared the city's patron saint, replacing the Greek St Theodore. Construction began almost immediately on the basilica which was completed in 832. Since then, additions have been made in different styles – Byzantine, Gothic and Renaissance, but the Oriental aspect,

St Mark's Square: Byron called it "the greatest drawing-room in Europe".

with its low cluster of domes and rich golden mosaics, predominates. Around the main doorway, bas-reliefs depict trades and the signs of the zodiac, while above it the mosaic shows the *Last Judgment*. Much of the interior decoration originated in the Eastern Mediterranean, some brought back after the Crusades, some created by Byzantine artists coming to work in Venice – marble paving, mosaic murals, icons, statues and, at the high altar, the 14th-century golden altar screen known as the Pala d'Oro. In the baptistery, see the *Dance of Salomé* in a 14th-century series relating the life of St John the Baptist, and in the narthex, a 13th-century *Creation of the World*. The Piazzetta dei Leoni, to the left of the basilica, is the gateway for visitors arriving from the Grand Canal, named after St Mark's emblematic red marble lions (1722). • **Daily 9.45am–5pm; Oct–Mar 9.45am– 4.45pm weekdays, Sun 2–4pm • Piazza San Marco**

Campanile di San Marco (F5) Almost 100 m (330 ft) high, the bell-tower stands proud of the rooftops and can be seen from afar. The existing tower was completed in 1912, its 12th-century predecessor having collapsed in 1902. A lift whisks you to the top for a superb view over the city and the Adriatic. • Daily 9am–7pm • Piazza San Marco

Museo Civico Correr (E5) Housed in the Ala Napoleonica and several rooms of the Procuratie Nuove, this museum presents an interesting collection of historical artefacts and documents about the Republic of Venice. Its Pinacoteca (art gallery) includes a *Pietà* by Antonello da Messina and some fine works by the Bellinis, Jacopo, Gentile and Giovanni. • Daily 9am–5pm; Apr–Oct 9am–7pm. Last entry one hour before closing time • Piazza San Marco 52

Museo Archeologico (F5) Directly adjoining the Correr in the Procuratie Nuove, the museum has an important collection of Greek sculpture, fragments

---

ITCHY FEET

Constantly on the move, the bold bronze chargers over the main portal of San Marco once crowned Trajan's Arch in Rome, but no one knows where they first came from. They later graced the imperial hippodrome of Constantinople, until Doge Dandolo took the city and the horses in 1204. In Venice they guarded the Arsenal for a while, then trotted over to San Marco. Napoleon, however, carted them off to Paris where they were harnessed to a chariot in the Tuileries Gardens; the Austrians brought them back. During both world wars, the horses were sent outside the city for safe-keeping. Afterwards the Venetians vowed that their horses would stay put. But a different kind of threat caused a change of plan. The horses had to be moved inside to preserve them from the effects of pollution, and replicas now stand on the balcony of the basilica.

of Roman sculpture and monuments, as well as Roman coins and marble statues. Most of the pieces were part of the personal collection donated by Cardinal Domenico Grimani in the 16th century. • Daily 8.15am–7.15pm; Apr–Oct 9am–7pm • Piazza San Marco 17

Biblioteca Nazionale Marciana (F5) Also accessible from the Corer, this great historic library was a major source of scholarship for the revolutionary wisdom of the Renaissance. Designed by Sansovino in the 16th century and decorated with works by Titian and Veronese, it is endowed with more than 900,000 volumes and 13,000 manuscripts. The Marciana includes among its treasures manuscripts by Petrarch, Marco Polo's testament and the Grimani Breviary (late 15th century), one of Europe's most precious illuminated texts. • Daily 9am–5pm; Apr–Oct 9am–7pm. Last entry 1h before closing time. • Piazza San Marco 13/A

Torre dell'Orologio (F5) Built between 1496 and 1499, and now completely restored, the clocktower is surmounted by two Moors, bronze figures which strike the hour on a large bell. The clock face marks the hours in Roman and Arabic numerals and with the signs of the zodiac. On January 6 (Epiphany) and on Ascension Day, the three Magi and a trumpeting angel emerge to revolve around a gilded Madonna. • Mercerie dell'Orologio

Palazzo Ducale (F5) The pink marble and white limestone Doges' Palace, 900 years old, was the seat of government, and also housed the law courts and the notorious prison cells. Originally a fortress,

FAMOUS FOOTSTEPS

Johann Wolfgang von Goethe

(1749–1832)
In his *Italian Journey*, Germany's best-known writer revelled in the anonymity of a stay in 1786 at a little boarding house near San Marco: "I can now really enjoy the solitude that I have often so longingly sighed for, since nowhere does one feel more alone than in a crowd where you push your way through, unknown by all."

it was rebuilt in is present Gothic style in the 14th and 15th centuries. Venice's greatest painters worked on the walls and ceilings: Tintoretto (see his magnificent *Paradise* in the Sala del Maggior Consiglio), Veronese in the Sala del Collegio, Palma il Giovane, Bassano and Titian. The Secret Itineraries tour takes you through rooms where, after looking at the terrifying paintings of Hieronymus Bosch, suspects were interrogated and tortured. • Daily 9am–5pm; Apr–Oct 9am–7pm. Last entry one hour before closing • Piazzetta San Marco

Ponte dei Sospiri (F5) Few prisoners in the world had such a beautiful walk to make as the baroque Bridge of Sighs linking the Doges' Palace and the prisons, built in 1600. Two parallel corridors lead to the staircase between the *piombi* (the cells under the lead-tiled roof), and the *pozzi* (in the cellars). As they passed the windows, the captives could see the lagoon – hence the name. Another more gruesome suggestion was that Sospiri was in fact an ironic understatement for the groans that could be heard from the torture chambers. • San Marco

San Zulian (F4) Also called San Giuliano, this is the only free-standing church in the city. It was founded in 829 but rebuilt in its present form by Sansovino in 1555. On the first altar to the right is Veronese's *Cristo morto*. • Campo San Zulian

San Salvador (E4) Its white façade festooned with statues by Bernardo Falcone, the three-naved church was consecrated in the 12th century and redesigned in the 16th. It has two paintings by Titian: *Annunziazione* (3rd altar on the right) and *Trasfigurazione* (high altar). In the adjacent cloisters, Telecom Italia has installed a Future Centre devoted to exhibitions of modern art and architecture. • Campo San Salvador

Ponte di Rialto (E4) Spanning the Grand Canal at its narrowest point, the white marble arch of the Rialto Bridge is one of the town's liveliest landmarks where pedestrians thread their way through boutiques selling jewellery, perfumes, clothing and sundry bric-a-brac. It is more imposing than elegant, since contractors preferred the modest bid of modest architect Antonio da Ponte ahead of Michelangelo, Palladio and Sansovino. • San Marco

Gran Teatro La Fenice (E5) In January 1996 a fire destroyed the interior of the sumptuous Venice Opera House. Like the phoenix of its name, it has risen anew from the flames and re-opened in November 2004 with a performance of La Traviata. The fire, which got out of control, was deliberately set by an electrician to cover up his inability to meet a renovation deadline – resulting in a seven-year jail sentence. • *Campo San Fantin 1977*

Scala Contarini del Bòvolo (E5) The Palace "of the Snail" takes its Venetian-dialect name from the spiralling staircase of its round tower, with decorative white balustrated arcades and little columns like icing on a cake. Climb the staircase to the dome for a splendid view. • *Apr–Oct 10am–6pm; Sat, Sun and winter months 10am–4pm* • *Corte dei Risi o del Bòvolo*

San Moisè (E5) Behind its extravagant Venetian-baroque façade, this single-nave church numbers among its more noteworthy artworks a *Washing of the Feet* by Tintoretto and *Last Supper* by Palma il Giovane. • *Campo San Moisè*

Santo Stefano (D5) With a huge treble-nave interior and a magnificent wooden ceiling, this is one of the major Gothic churches in the city. Its art treasures include in the Sacristy Bartolomeo Vivarini's *St Lawrence and St Nicholas of Bari*, an important older Venetian painting, Paolo Veneziano's *Crucifixion* (1348), and three works by Tintoretto. • *Campo San Stefano (F. Morosini)*

Mercatino Antiquariato (D5) The grey-paved square in front of San Maurizio church is the site of a charming antiques fair usually held at Christmas, Easter and during the Regata Storica (dates change so check with the Tourist Office). • *Campo San Maurizio*

Palazzo Grassi (D5) The palace has been beautifully renovated to house the modern art collections of French businessman François Pinaut (including Keith Haring, Damien Hirst, Jeff Koons), displayed in temporary exhibitions. • *Daily 10am–7pm* • *Campo San Samuele 3231*

Ponte dell'Accademia (D5) Built across the Grand Canal in 1934 to replace an earlier iron bridge, this wooden structure has been reinforced with steel.

SHOPPING IN SAN MARCO

Venice is a dream for shoppers, full of exquisite and irresistible boutiques selling everything from postcards to hand-made glassware from Murano. Prices are quite steep, but this is Venice, after all. Shops are generally open from 9am until 12.30pm and from 3 to 7.30pm. In summer, they stay open during the lunch hour and on Sundays.

The most exclusive shops cluster around Piazza San Marco, while the main shopping streets, the Mercerie (do Aprile and San Salvador, E4), are lined with appealing boutiques with more competitive prices. One of the most distinguished addresses to look out for is **Jesurum** on the piazza itself, lacemarkers since 1870 (the fascinating history of this shop is recounted in detail on www.jesurum.it). The even older **Missiaglia**, which sells watches, jewellery and handmade objets d'art in gold, silver and precious stones was founded in 1846. **Codognato**, Calle Seconda a l'Ascension 1295, is well-known for heavy, richly decorated jewellery, both antique and modern. In a palace on Calle Longa 4391/A, **Pauly & Co** offers a sophisticated collection of hats, glasses, furniture and marble objects. Their second shop in Piazza San Marco sells Murano glassware, vases, light-fittings and lampshades. You'll find more glassware at **Venini**, Piazzetta dei Leoncini 314, or **Veneziartigiani**, Calle Larga 412/3, a cooperative for Venetian craftsmen also making objects in paper, as well as costume jewellery and masks.

If it's art books you're after, don't miss **Fantoni Libri d'Arte**, Salizzada San Luca 4121 – the most complete art bookshop in the historic centre of

Venice, mostly in Italian but they do also stock some English books on Venice and Italian food. To jot down your impressions of this lovely floating city, call in at **Il Papiro**, Calle del Piovan 2764, overflowing with writing materials; paper, pens, inks and notebooks. The city's oldest bookbindery, **Antica Legatoria Piazzesi**, on Campo della Feltrina, no longer produces its beautiful hand-printed paper except to order, but you will find it hard to resist the fabulous marbled creations of **Ebrû** (a Turkish word meaning "cloudy"), a stationery shop on Campo Santo Stefano (see its history on www.albertovalese-ebru.com).

For the quirkiest leather shoes visit **Daniela Ghezzo Segalin Venezia** on Calle dei Fuseri, and do not miss the extraordinary sculptures of everyday objects in wood (from lace to life-size cars) by **Livio De Marchi** in his gallery on Salizzada San Samuele near the Palazzo Grassi.

WALKING TOUR: SAN MARCO

At the far end of the Piazza San Marco, directly opposite the Basilica, walk through the central arcade in the **Ala Napoleonica**, originally planned by Napoleon Bonaparte as a grand ballroom, now the entrance to the Museo Correr. On Calle Bocca di Piazza, pass between the Post Office and 13th-century **Palazzo Salvadego** (with a smart ground-floor men's boutique) to turn left on busy **Frezzeria** (Arrowsmith's Street). Go right on Salizzada San Moise over the bridge to the flashy Baroque **Chiesa San Moisè**, commemorating with a tombstone the dodgy Scottish financier John Law (1671–1729), who was bankrupted after founding France's first bank. Continue west past fashionable boutiques on **Calle Larga XXII Marzo** (the date of Venice's short-lived 1848 expulsion of the Austrians). Turn right on Calle delle Veste to the beautiful **Gran Teatro La Fenice**, resurrected home of Venetian opera. Opposite is the Sansovino's late-Renaissance **Chiesa San Fantín**. At the rear of the Campo is the **Ateneo Veneto** academy of science and letters (another Napoleonic project), crowned by the Virgin Mary and two archangels.

Walk around La Fenice and over the canal along the aptly renamed **Fondamenta Maria Callas** to take Calle del Piovan to **Chiesa Santa Maria del Giglio** (St Mary of the Lily). The Baroque façade's statues lean obligingly forward to be more visible to passers-by. Down by the Grand Canal is the equally grand **Gritti Palace** hotel. Double back to the church and go left over two canal bridges to **Campo San Maurizio** with its four palazzi, Gothic **Zaguri** (2631) and **Molin** (2758) and neoclassical **Bellavite** (2760) and **Da Ponte** (2746).

Calle del Spezier leads left to cafés and the fine Gelateria Paolin on the popular **Campo San Stefano** (scene of Venice's last bullfight, in 1802). It is surrounded by some handsome palazzi, notably **Loredan-Mocenigo** (2945) in the southwest corner. Continue past the Palladian façade of **Chiesa San Vidal** to the **Accademia Bridge**.

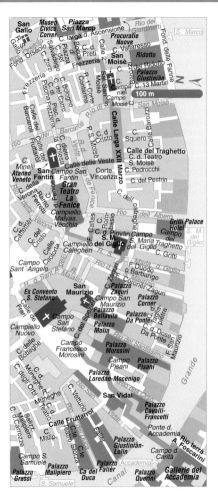

From Piazza San Marco via La Fenice opera house to the Accademia Bridge, take in some handsome palazzi, churches, smart shops and good ice cream cafés.

Start:
Vaporetto San Marco (Vallaresso)

Finish:
Vaporetto Accademia

GRAND CANAL CRUISE

All visitors to Venice have to follow the Grand Canal (B 3–E 6) to reach their final destination. Board a vaporetto and glide past the ribbon of Byzantine, Gothic, baroque, Renaissance and neoclassical palaces and historic buildings hemming both sides of the Canalazzo from Piazzale Roma or the Santa Lucia railway station all the way to San Marco, opposite the Dogana da Mar.

Here, in order, are the principal historic buildings you'll see along the route. For the churches and palaces that are open for visits, you'll find further details in the relevant chapters of this guide.

When the railway station was built in the 1950s, a church and several palaces were demolished to clear space for it. The only survivor was the **Chiesa degli Scalzi**, a baroque church which the Roman community of Discalced Carmelites commissioned from the architect Longhena in 1654. "Discalced" means barefooted, though the nuns and friars actually wore sandals. Before your boat passes beneath the Ponte degli Scalzi, look out for the **Chiesa di San Simeone Piccolo** (18th century), crowned with a large copper dome.

On your right after the first bend in the canal you will see the **Fondaco dei Turchi**, an old Venetian-Byzantine palace which, after 1621, was a warehouse for Turkish and other merchants of the Ottoman Empire. On your left, the Renaissance-style **Palazzo Vendramin-Calergi** was the last home of the composer Richard Wagner. It is the winter quarters of the municipal Casino.

Look again to the right. Next to the **Chiesa San Stae**, founded in the 10th century and dedicated to Saint Eustace, you'll see a small building with a red façade which was once the headquarters of the guild of drawers and spinners of gold.

A little further on, the imposing **Ca' Pesaro**, perhaps the most handsome baroque palace in Venice, houses the museums of Oriental Art and Modern Art.

The **Ca' Corner della Regina** dates from the 18th century and was built on the site of the house where Caterina Cornaro was born in 1454: she became the Queen of Cyprus upon her marriage to Jacques II of Lusignan.

The **Ca' d'Oro** (left bank), a delicate mingling of Byzantine and Gothic, contains the art collections of Baron Franchetti, bequeathed to the Venetian Municipality in 1916. You are now approaching the Rialto. The fish market is held each morning in the **Pescheria**, a square building in neo-Gothic style on the right bank. Next, together with an open-air fruit and vegetable market, come the long façades of the **Fabbriche Nuove** and **Fabbriche Vecchie**, originally commercial buildings and today housing the Law Courts.

Standing on the left bank just before the Rialto Bridge, the **Fondaco dei Tedeschi** was a warehouse reserved for German traders, now a post office. Along the left bank after the bridge, there is a succession of prestigious palaces. The **Palazzo Dolfin Manin**, built in 1550, today serves as the head office of the Bank of Italy.

The **Palazzo Bembo**, with Gothic windows, dates from the 15th century. **Ca' Loredan** and **Ca' Farsetti**, both built in the 13th century, together form the Town Hall.

Almost opposite the **Palazzo Grimani**, a sumptuous Renaissance dwelling, the **Palazzo Papadopoli** (right bank) was constructed in the 15th century for a family of jewellers. Next door, the **Palazzo della Madonnetta** has retained a pretty 15th-century bas-relief of the Virgin and Child.

Further along on the left, the **Palazzi Mocenigo**, a group of four buildings in Istrian stone from the 16th and 17th centuries, provided inspiration for Lord Byron, who began work on *Don Juan* when he stayed here in 1818. The neighbouring palace, **Palazzo Contarini delle Figure**, from the early 16th century, owes its name to the caryatids holding up the balcony. It was the Venice home for architect Andrea Palladio.

Located on a bend of the canal and bordering the Rio di Ca' Foscari, the **Palazzo Balbi** dates from the Renaissance but has some baroque decoration on the façade. It is the seat of the regional council of Venetia. Opposite, the magnificent Gothic **Ca' Foscari** is home to the University.

On your left, next to the small church of **San Samuele**, whose square tower dates from the 12th century, stands the **Palazzo Grassi**, which has undergone extensive renovation to house a major modern art collection.

The **Ca' Rezzonico** opposite provides a noble home for the Museum of Decorative Arts. This palace remained unfinished for almost a century following the death of the architect Longhena during its construction.

As you approach the **Ponte dell'Accademia**, a wooden bridge with a single span, you will see on your right the prestigious **Gallerie dell' Accademia**, the Academy of Fine Arts. Further on, **Ca' Venier dei Leoni**, lower than its neighbours, is in fact an unfinished palace, bought by Peggy Guggenheim to house her collection of modern paintings. It is said that in the 18th century the Venier family kept a lion tethered in the courtyard, hence the name of their palace. The huge **Palazzo Corner**, also known as Ca' Grande, was built by Sansovino in 1537. Today it is the Prefecture of Venice.

Looking once more at the right bank, you see the attractive **Palazzo Dario** (1487) with its Renaissance façade overlaid with polychrome marble. Soon you come upon the superb **Basilica of Santa Maria della Salute**, a masterpiece by Longhena, built in 1630 in gratitude for the salvation the Virgin was believed to have brought from a plague epidemic.

At the end of the **Dogana da Mar**, the old customs houses on the right bank promontory, the waterway opens into Saint Mark's canal. On the Dogana's belfry, two bronze figures support a golden sphere surmounted by the statue of Fortune.

Finally, you arrive at the **Piazza San Marco**, and it is time to come back down to earth and explore the wonderful realities of this living fantasy.

GONDOLAS

These distinctive boats have been negotiating the canals since the 11th century. In olden days, wealthy Venetians used to paint their gondolas in bright colours and adorn them with rich decoration. Rivalry among the nobles as to who had the finest gondola reached such a point that in 1562 the government enacted a law decreeing that all gondolas must be plain black, and they have stayed that way – now spruced up with an occasional discreet touch of white, siver or gilt paint and some velvet cushions. The S-shape of the *ferro* adorning the bow is said to represent the bends of the Grand Canal, with six prongs for the six *sestieri* and a rounded top like the doge's hat. The curvy oarlock is called a *forcola*. Until the 19th century there were some 10,000 gondolas, but now only 500 remain, usually used to punt tourists around the city or ferry them across the Grand Canal.

DORSODURO

Cross over the Ponte dell'Accademia to enter the sestiere of Dorsoduro, the intellectual district, with the University, museums, public and private collections and foundations. In the southern part of Venice, it is a quiet residential area, considered to be one of the most pleasant places in which to live – described in a fine 20th-century novel, *Dorsoduro*, by one of its residents Pier Maria Pasinetti (1913–2006).

THE DISTRICT AT A GLANCE

🏛 **SIGHTS**

Architecture
Santa Maria
della Salute★ 35

I Gesuati 36

San Sebastiano★ 37

Sant'Angelo
Raffaele..................37

San Nicoló
dei Mendicoli..........37

Scuola Grande dei
Carmini 37

Santa Maria del
Carmelo 38

Ponte dei Pugni 38

San Pantalon 38

Art
Gallerie
dell'Accademia★ ...34

Collezione Peggy
Guggenheim★ 35

Collezione
Vittorio Cini 35

Ca' Rezzonico★ 38

Atmosphere
Zattere★ 35

Rio di San Trovaso★ .36

Campo Santa
Margherita★ 38

Campiello Mosca 39

🚶 **WALKING
TOUR   40**

☕ **WINING AND
DINING   79**

Gallerie dell'Accademia (D6) The splendid Academy galleries are housed in the old buildings of Santa Maria della Carità, a combination of church, monastery and school. This extensive collection of Venetian art was begun in 1807. All the great Venetian painters are represented, but the highlights are Giorgione's *La Tempesta*, Giovanni Bellini's *Pietà* and several versions of *Madonna col Bambino*, Lorenzo Lotto's *Ritratto di Gentiluomo*, Titian's *Presentazione della Vergine al Tempio*, Veronese's *Il convito in casa di Levi* and Tintoretto's *Miracolo di San Marco*. • Mon 8.15am–2pm; Tues–Sun 8.15am– 7.15pm • Campo della Carità 1050

Collezione Peggy Guggenheim (D6) The American collector Peggy Guggenheim lived for 30 years in the Palazzo Venier dei Leoni, whichnow displays to the public her collection of European and American avant-garde artworks. The most important are the works of Max Ernst and Jackson Pollock. • Daily (except Tues) 10am–6pm • Calle San Gregorio 701

Collezione Vittorio Cini (D6) Occupying two floors of a Renaissance palace, this is a collection of antique furniture, objets d'art and – rare in Venice – paintings of the Tuscan school from the 13th to 15th centuries (Daddi, Lippi, Piero della Francesca, Pontormo). • Daily (except Mon) 10am–6pm • Campo San Vio

Santa Maria della Salute (E6) The Baroque church completed in 1687 is regarded as Baldassare Longhena's supreme achievement, justly earning its place as a landmark on the city's skyline rivalling San Marco itself. A solemn festival commemorates annually (November 21) the Virgin Mary's deliverance of the city from a plague in 1630. Major works of Titian and Tintoretto adorn the altars, ceiling and walls of the Sacristy. • Campo della Salute

Zattere (E6) Bordering the Giudecca Canal, this long quay runs along the south side of Dorsoduro, from the Punta della Dogana (Customs Point) as far as San Basegio. Used from the 17th century as the unloading point for the wood that was floated down the Piave river to Venice, it used to be an area of intense commercial activity. Today it is a most

In the narrowest of alleys you'll discover tiny gardens catching the sunlight.

pleasant promenade, sunny and sheltered from the gusts of the bora wind, offering lovely views of the island of La Giudecca from its café terraces. The ice cream parlour on Rio Terrà ai Saloni is renowned for its *gianduiotto* – chocolate, honey, hazelnuts and cream.

I Gesuati (D6) Also called Santa Maria del Rosario, the church was built between 1724 and 1736 with donations from the people of Venice. The interior is a veritable gallery for the sculptor Giovanni Maria Morlaiter, along with paintings by Tiepolo, Piazzetta and Tintoretto. • **Fondamenta Zattere ai Gesuati**

Rio di San Trovaso (C6–D5) Patrician palaces, some dating back to the 14th century, line the quays of this waterway linking the Grand and Giudecca canals. The Palazzo Contarini degli Scrigni is made up of two buildings, one with a Gothic façade, the other 17th century. Other noteworthy buildings are the Giustinian-Recanati, Nani and Sangiantoffetti palaces. Closer to the Giudecca Canal, the Squero di San Trovaso is one of the last Venetian boatworks still actively repairing and building gondolas.

San Sebastiano (B5) Paolo Veronese took refuge in this church in 1555 after fleeing Verona where he had committed a murder. In gratitude, he covered the interior with a masterly series of wall-paintings, including a splendid series in trompe-l'œil on the ceiling of the nave, telling the Biblical story of Esther. Veronese is buried near the organ. • Campo San Sebastiano

Sant'Angelo Raffaele (B5) Designed on the form of a Greek cross, the church – one of Venice's oldest – was rebuilt in the 17th century. A sculpted group on the portal shows the Archangel Raphael and Tobias; inside, five panels by Gianantonio Guardi depict episodes of the life of Tobias. • Campo Angelo Raffaele

San Nicolò dei Mendicoli (B5) In the heart of a humble district of fishermen and artisans, this church ("of the beggars") is little changed since its 7th-century origins. The porch, which used to be a shelter for the poor, is typical of that period. • Campo San Nicolò dei Mendicoli

Scuola Grande dei Carmini (C5) The Venetian *scuole* were not schools but meeting places, like social clubs, for confraternities formed by groups of citizens who shared a common origin or profession. This building with two façades, completed by Longhena in 1670, was the headquarters of a pres-

FAMOUS FOOTSTEPS

John Ruskin
(1819–1900)
A plaque on the Zattere ai Gesuati commemorates the controversial Victorian art-historian, author of *The Stones of Venice* as the *Sacerdote dell'Arte nelle nostre Pietre* (High Priest of Art in our Stones). Author Jan Morris wrote: "Everywhere he went, people wondered in puzzlement whether he was a madman or a scholar."

tigious confraternity dedicated to the Virgin of Carmel, which was founded in Palestine in the 13th century and to which men were admitted only from 1595. By 1675 it had expanded to 75,000 members. Inside, see the staircase painted in grisaille, the richly decorated ceilings (one by Tiepolo, *La Vergina in Gloria*), and an interesting *Judith and Holofernes* by Giambattista Piazzetta in the Archives room. • Daily 9am–6pm; Sat and winter months 9am–4pm • Campo dei Santa Margherita 2617

Santa Maria del Carmelo (I Carmini) (C5) Enlarged and altered several times since the 14th century, the church has gilded statues in the nave and many admirable paintings by Cima da Conegliano *(Adoration of the Shepherds)*, Giorgio Martini and Lorenzo Lotto. • Campo dei Carmini

Campo Santa Margherita (C5) The social hub of Dorsoduro, this tree-lined campo has always been a market place and remains the biggest and liveliest in the city. It is lined by rather modest houses and a couple of fading palaces which still bear traces of their former Byzantine or Gothic glory. Next to the derelict church is a bell tower with a baroque marble dragon at the base.

Ponte dei Pugni (C5) Walk along the Fondamenta Gherardini to the Bridge of Fists, so called because it was the site of fist-fights between boxers of rival factions standing on a spot marked by two pairs of footprints in the marble. There are no balustrades so it was easy to heave the losing contender straight into the canal. Beneath the bridge is a large shop-boat selling vegetables.

Ca' Rezzonico (C–D5) Designed by Longhena, this large baroque palace on the Grand Canal houses an exceptional collection of paintings, objets d'art and furniture in the Museo del Settecento, to show you what life was like for the wealthy in the 18th century. There are ceiling paintings by Tiepolo, and the ball-room is simply dazzling. • Daily (except Tues) Apr–Oct 10am–6pm; winter months 10am–5pm. Last entry one hour before closing • San Barnaba 3136

San Pantalon (C4) Already important in the 11th century, the church is famed for the ceiling painting of the nave, made up of 40 canvases (1680–1704) by Giovanni Antonio Fumiani, illustrating the martyrdom and glory of St Pantaleon, court physician to Emperor Galerius and put to death under Diocletian. Other works to be seen are by Paolo Veronese and Palma il Giovane, and there is a splendid *Coronation of the Virgin* (1444) attributed to Antonio Vivarini and Giovanni d'Alemagna. • **Campo San Pantalon**

Campiello Mosca (C4) Behind San Pantalon, this little square owes its name to the many workshops that manufactured *mosche* (flies), the black taffeta beauty spots which ladies used to stick on their face to emphasize the whiteness of their skin (or to disguise blemishes).

THE SCENE OF THE CRIME

The dark side of Venice – its dank cellars and decaying palaces, its slime-green cuttings and shadow-cloaked alleys – forms an unquiet backdrop for many a tale of murder and mystery. The city's enigmatic atmosphere plays the leading rôle in Donna Leon's series featuring the dapper Commissario Guido Brunetti – *Death at La Fenice, A Venetian Reckoning, Alta Aqua, The Anonymous Venetian,* and so on. It arouses ardent love and pain in Jeanette Winterson's *The Passion*, obsessive desire in Thomas Mann's *Death in Venice*, and unleashes psychic powers in Daphne du Maurier's *Don't Look Now*. The 19th-century novel by Wilkie Collins, *The Haunted Hotel*, is shrouded in melodrama and suspense. For something more light-hearted, delve into *The Case of the Orphaned Bassoonists*, investigated by Barbara Wilson's witty accidental detective Cassandra Reilly.

WALKING TOUR: DORSODURO

From the majestic **Basilica di Santa Maria della Salute**, almost as much an emblem as San Marco opposite, walk out to **Punta della Dogana**, where the 17th-century customs warehouses are to be used for temporary art exhibitions. On the corner tower, two bronze Atlas giants support a golden ball and the figure of Fortune. Double back past the Salute over the canal bridge of former Abbazia di San Gregorio along Calle Bastion to Campiello Barbaro. Stop on Ponte San Cristoforo to view the late-Gothic rear façade of **Palazzo Dario** and its garden with a wall-plaque commemorating French poet Henri de Régnier (1864–1936). Calle San Cristoforo leads to the unfinished 18th-century **Palazzo Venier dei Leoni**, now home of the Peggy Guggenheim Collection of modern art. South of Calle San Cristoforo, take Sottoportego e Corte Molin and turn right on Rio Terrà San Vio and Calle Navaro past some typical 17th-century Dorsoduro houses and bourgeois *palazzetti* on and around **Calle delle Mende**, notable for the distinctive herringbone-patterned paving.

Cross the bridge and turn left on Calle della Chiesa, over a second bridge, then left again on Fondamenta Venier beside Rio di San Vio to the **Zattere** quays facing La Giudecca. Turn right along the promenade past the Dominicans' 18th-century **Chiesa dei Gesuati** (or Santa Maria del Rosario). After the bridge over Rio San Trovaso, turn right and left for a view from the next bridge over the **Squero San Trovaso** boatyard, where boatmen-carpenters can still be seen building and repairing their vessels in one of Venice's last gondola workshops. Back on the Zattere, continue past *palazzi* housing offices of the Venice port authority, noting for later the unusually good waterfront **Ae Oche** pizzeria. Turn right at the San Basilio vaporetto station, take Fondamenta San Basegio (Basilio) to the second bridge and cross to 16th-century **Chiesa San Sebastiano**, architecturally unprepossessing treasure trove for Veronese's splendid wall and ceiling paintings.

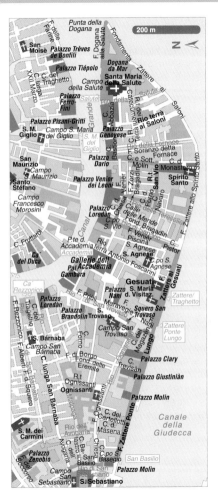

One of the Venetians' own favourite walks: from the Salute through characteristic residential quarters and along the airy Zattere quays on the Giudecca Canal.

Start:
Vaporetto Salute

Finish:
Vaporetto San Basilio

SANTA CROCE

The eastern part of this district has retained its old palaces looking out over the Grand Canal. This is where people do most of their sightseeing, because on the western side, the old houses have been demolished and replaced by an industrial zone, the port and Piazzale Roma, a vast car park.

THE DISTRICT AT A GLANCE

🏛 **SIGHTS**

Architecture
Santa Maria Mater
Domini 42

San Stae 43

San Giacomo
dell'Orio ★ 43

Ponte degli Scalzi.....43

San Nicoló
da Tolentino 43

Art
Ca' Pesaro ★ 42

Museum
Museo Civico di Storia
Naturale 43

🚶 **WALKING
TOUR   44**

☕ **WINING AND
DINING   79**

Ca' Pesaro (D3) The Modern Art Gallery *(Galleria d'Arte Moderna)* occupies rooms in one of the most famous of Venetian palaces on the Grand Canal. It was founded in 1897 to display a series of works from the Biennale exhibitions, and now comprises a fine collection of Italian and foreign paintings, sculptures and drawings from the end of the 19th century until the present day. Among the artists represented here are Arp, Chagall, De Chirico, Kandinsky, Klee, Klimt, Miró and Moore. In the Museum of Oriental Art *(Museo d'Arte Orientale)*, you can admire a collection of Japanese art from the Edo period (1614–1868). Other sections are devoted to China and Indonesia. Many visitors come here to admire the architecture of the palace rather than its art. • **Daily (except Mon)** 10am– 6pm; winter months 10am–5pm Tel. 041 524 06 95 • Fondamenta di Ca' Pesaro 2070

Santa Maria Mater Domini (D3) Behind Ca' Pesaro, this Renaissance-style church with a simple and elegant interior is adorned with admirable works by

Vincenzo Catena and Tintoretto. The church stands on an attractive *campo*, regular in shape and with pleasing proportions; it is lined with some splendid Byzantine and Gothic buildings. Note in particular the 13th-century Casa Zane (no. 2174), Casa Viaro-Zane (nos. 2120–22) and the 14th century Casa Barbaro (no. 2177). • **Campo Santa Maria Mater Domini**

San Stae (D3) Rebuilt in the 17th century in Palladian style, the church is dedicated to St Eustace, a Roman general who, when out hunting, was converted to Christianity by a vision of a stag with a luminous crucifix between its antlers. The church is used for temporary exhibitions and concerts. Inside you can see works by Piazzetta, Tiepolo and de Ricci. • **Campo San Stae**

San Giacomo dell'Orio (D3) On a tree-shaded square that makes a pleasant summer setting for shows and festivals, the church was built in the 9th and 10th centuries and modified in 1225 and again in the early 15th century, when various Gothic elements were added. Its art treasures include works by Paolo Veneziano, Lorenzo Lotto and Veronese. The brick bell tower dates from the 1225 reconstruction. • **Campo San Giacomo dell'Orio**

Museo Civico di Storia Naturale (D3) The Natural History Museum, a small collection of fossils, mammals, minerals and marine fauna, is housed in a 13th-century Venetian-Byzantine building that was originally an inn and warehouse for Turkish and other merchants of the Ottoman Empire. • **Tues–Fri 9am–1pm, Sat, Sun 10am–4pm** • **Salizzada del Fondaco dei Turchi 1730**

Ponte degli Scalzi (C3) The most recent of the Grand Canal's bridges linking Santa Croce with the Cannaregio sestiere and Santa Lucia railway station was renovated in 1934 by Eugenio Miozzi, replacing an iron structure built by the Austrians in 1858. • **Santa Croce**

San Nicolò da Tolentino (C4) Consecrated in 1602, the church stands on an unusual campo which gives onto a *rio* (a small canal). The façade with a colonnaded portal was added in the 18th century. The next-door monastery is now the seat of Venice's Faculty of Architecture. • **Campo et Campazzo dei Tolentini**

WALKING TOUR: SANTA CROCE

To the right of the white marble Baroque **Chiesa di San Stae** (St Eustace), take Salizzada San Stae past 17th-century **Palazzo Mocenigo**, *not* the one Lord Byron lived in, located on the Grand Canal, but housing the Museo dei Tessuti e dei Costumi (an opulent collection of textiles and costumes). Turn left on Calle del Tintor (appropriately, the Textile-Dyers Street) over a bridge and left again along the canal on Fondamenta Rimpetto Mocenigo. Turn right on Calle Pesaro to **Ca' Pesaro**, home of the Modern Art and Oriental Art museums. It is well worth taking a peep at its beautiful white stone courtyard before returning along Fondamenta Pesaro, then left and first right on Calle dei Tiozzi.

This leads to **Campo Santa Maria Mater Domini** with its Renaissance church and medieval houses – 13th-century **Ca' Zane** (2174) and the 14th-century **Palazzetto Viaro-Zane** (2123) and **Casa Barbaro** (2179). From Calle della Chiesa, which becomes Calle di Cristo, turn right on Calle di Scaletèr across Rio Terrà Secondo to the 15th-century Gothic **Palazzo Soranzo-Pisani** (2278). Left of the Palazzo, Rio Terrà Prima crosses a canal to Calle del Tintor, leading into the airy **Campo San Giacomo dell'Orio**, popular with neighbourhood families. The ancient church, originally 9th century, is surrounded by shady plane trees, shops and pleasant cafés.

Go north on Calle Larga and zigzag left on Calle Spezier to the street called Fontego dei Turchi, leading to the **Fontego** (or Fondaco) **dei Turchi**, once a warehouse for the Ottoman Empire's Turkish, Bosnian and Albanian merchants and now the Natural History Museum (Museo di Storia Naturale). Double back on the Salizzada to turn right on Calle del Capitello over to the quiet little **Campo San Zan Degola** (San Giovanni Decollato, St John Beheaded). From Calle Bembo, turn right on Rio Terrà over to **Riva di Biasio** for its fine view across the Grand Canal to Cannaregio's Palazzo Labia and Chiesa di San Geremia.

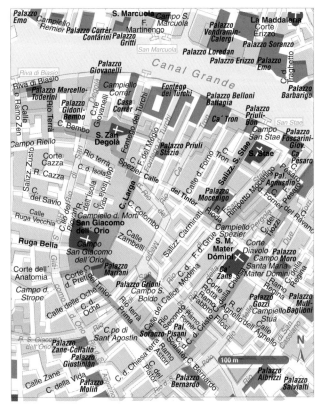

Behind Santa Croce's Grand Canal palazzi, explore its historic squares, Campo Santa Maria Mater Domini, San Giacomo dell'Orio and San Zan Degola.

Start: Vaporetto San Stae

Finish: Vaporetto Riva di Biasio

PAINTING

What is it that makes the painting of Venice so quintessentially "Venetian"? Alone among Italy's major centres of culture, Venice faced the eastern Mediterranean and the powerful influence of Byzantine art. After the Crusaders' conquest of Constantinople in 1204, the Venetian fleet ferried back with its customary cargoes of exotic Oriental riches a team of **Greek mosaicists** to work with local artists on the Basilica of San Marco. Together with the Orient's shimmering fabrics, precious stones and enamels, the mosaics ushered in Venice's enduring taste for brilliant colour, enhanced by the magic light bouncing off the Adriatic.

Byzantine inspiration was evident in the refined elegance of **Paolo Veneziano** (1290–c.1358), notably in his polyptych of Jesus, Mary and the life of St Mark (the *Pala feriale*), commissioned by Dandolo to cover the basilica's Pala d'Oro on weekdays, and now in San Marco's Museo Marciano. **Antonio Vivarini** (active 1440–76) in his monumental *Coronation of the Virgin* (San Pantalon) added to Byzantine formality a wealth of International Gothic detail learned from Gentile da Fabriano.

Venetian art's major breakthrough came with the Bellini family. **Jacopo Bellini** (c.1400–70) was the founding father through his sons Gentile and Giovanni, while marrying his daughter to the great Andrea Mantegna. Jacopo's own paintings (*Madonna and Child*, Accademia) offered a strong realism, but it was his sketchbooks (now in the British Museum and Louvre) that had most influence on his sons and son-in-law. **Gentile Bellini** (c.1429–1507) thrived on grand ceremonial subjects such as the *Procession of the True Cross* for the Scuola Grande di San Giovanni Evangelista, now displayed in the Accademia. His brother

Gentile Bellini: Procession of the True Cross (Processione in Piazza San Marco)

Giovanni Bellini (c. 1430–1516) was Venice's first great Renaissance master, with a body of work as *Serenissima* as the city itself. From brother-in-law Andrea Mantegna, he acquired a keen sense of crisp detail, firm line and sculptured forms, adding a distinctive humanity to the *Madonna and Child* triptych (Accademia). "Giambellini" gave full rein to his poetic nature as the Venetian pioneer of oil painting, following the visit of Sicilian master Antonello da Messina. Oils gave a new warmth to his colour, softer flesh tones and a harmony of light and form, with great emotional effect in two versions of an *Enthroned Madonna* for the Frari and San Giobbe (now in the Accademia). Age did not dull the sensitivity of such later paintings as his sun-filled *Madonna and Child Between John the Baptist and Catherine* (Accademia) and *Enthroned Madonna with Saints* (San Zaccaria).

Stylistically, **Vittore Carpaccio** (1460–1526) had nothing in common with the Bellini clan except, superficially perhaps, the crowded canvases of Gentile, with whom he competed for lucrative deals with the confraternities. His story-telling skills brought a witty, personal manner and minute detail to the *Legend of St Ursula* (Accademia), eight scenes commissioned by the Scuola di Sant'Orsola.

The few paintings left by Giovanni Bellini's pupil **Giorgione**, appropriately "Great George" (c. 1478–1510), heightened the enigma of his genius. His landscapes were neither sentimental nor naturalistic, his very human portraits warm and radiant, independent of any Florentine influence. The luminous colour and rich textures made him the supreme exponent of the "Venetian" essence of Venetian painting. With its nude

Giovanni Bellini: Enthroned Madonna (Pala di San Giobbe)

Carpaccio: Arrival of the Ambassadors, from the legend of St Ursula (Arrivo degli ambasciatori). Detail.

mother bathed in the surreal light of a hostile nature, the celebrated *Tempest* (Accademia) offered no demonstrable Biblical or mythological reference, epitomizing his sublime mystery.

A longer, immensely prosperous life enabled **Titian** (c. 1487–1576) to be an untiringly prolific if perhaps less original genius than Giorgione, with whom he worked on several (now lost) frescoes and whose influence he showed throughout his career. The emotional power, in turn cosmic, erotic and existential, of his own undoubted greatness inspired Tintoretto and Veronese, but Rubens and Velazquez, too. His revolutionary brushwork enhanced tactile surfaces, volume and detail, but also rendered colour more vigorous and dynamic. In his monumental *Assumption of the Madonna* altarpiece for the Frari, Mary is a very physical, not at all ethereal figure. Lively cherubs and sturdy Apostles – like the Accademia's muscular *John the Baptist* – recall characters familiar to his country youth on the Veneto mainland. Realism and compassion infuse portraits of doges, kings and popes. Depiction of female beauty might be ideal or sensual, in variations on the Venus theme (Madrid, London and New York), or both, in *Mary Magdalene* (Hermitage, St Petersburg).

Lorenzo Lotto (1480–1556) is a case apart. Travelling widely on the mainland, he responded both to Venetian contemporaries and to Roman Mannerism, while imposing his eccentric personality. Religious subjects, *St Nicolas* (Santa Maria dei Carmini) and *Sant'Antonio Giving Alms* (San Giovanni e Paolo), were intensely lyrical, but always psychologically complex. The piercing introspection of portraits – *Young Gentleman in his Study* (Accademia) – is often startlingly modern.

Tintoretto (1518–94) was an endlessly ambitious artist. He won the commission for *Scenes of the Passion* at the Scuola Grande di San Rocco by sneaking in to install overnight a completed ceiling painting instead of the scale model specified by competition rules. Working at lightning speed, he had no patience for Titian's deliberate approach. Vivid results expressed rapid action and passionate emotion, achieved by a characteristic blaze of colour and movement in his *San Marco* paintings (Accademia). This devout Christian's work for San Rocco, particularly the huge *Crucifixion*, was a profound meditation on the life of Christ.

Born and trained in Verona, the magnificent **Paolo Veronese** (1528–88) came to Venice in 1553. He was worldly rather than spiritual in treating Biblical themes, with a taste for sumptuous festivities in marble palaces for aristocrats in velvets, satins, silks and brocades. Averting the Inquisition's outrage at what seemed like a sacrilegious depiction of *The Last Supper*, he made a few changes and renamed it *Feast in the House of Levi* (Accademia). Nor is there much mystical about *The Mystical Marriage of St Catherine* (Accademia) with a Catherine more wealthy princess than austere saint. And he really went to town with *The Triumph of Venice* for the Doge's Palace.

Tiepolo (1692–1770) topped off the Venetian pageant with a profusion of grand paintings produced on an industrial scale. Strongly influenced by Veronese, this brilliant colourist displayed humour and extravagant heroics in his ceiling frescoes for Ca' Rezzonico and Palazzo Labia.

Veronese: Feast in the House of Levi (Cena in casa di Levi)

SAN POLO

In the centre of Venice, this is the smallest of the *sestieri*, containing many churches and great *scuole,* as well as the Rialto, one of the first inhabited areas of the city. From the 10th century until the present day it has been a trading centre.

THE DISTRICT AT A GLANCE

🏛 **SIGHTS**	Santa Maria Gloriosa dei Frari ★ 51	**Atmosphere** Rialto Markets ★ 52
Architecture San Rocco 50	San Polo 52	**Museums** Casa Goldoni............52
Scuola Grande di San Rocco ★ 50	Palazzo Albrizzi.........52	
Scuola Grande di San Giovanni Evangelista ★ 50	Ponte delle Tette ......52 San Giacomo di Rialto 53	👫 **WALKING TOUR 54** ☕ **WINING AND DINING 80**

San Rocco (C4) Begun in 1489, the church is consecrated to Saint Roch, born in Montpellier, France and believed to offer protection against the plague – a chronic Venetian preoccupation. He is shown in bas-relief on the façade, the work of the sculptor Morlaiter. Inside, several paintings by Tintoretto illustrate episodes from the life of the saint. • Campo San Rocco

Scuola Grande di San Rocco (C4) The institution of San Rocco was intended to help plague victims, and construction of the building began in 1489. Four architects worked on it in succession over a century. It is mainly known for the magnificent cycle of San Rocco paintings, more than 50 paintings executed by Tintoretto from 1564 to 1587, generally regarded as his finest work. • Daily 9am–5.30pm • Campo di San Rocco 3054

Scuola Grande di San Giovanni Evangelista (C4) In a charming little square opposite the little church of the same name, this scuola was built between the 14th and 16th centuries. Above the marble Renaissance portal is an eagle, the symbol of St John the Evangelist. Inside you can admire paintings by Tintoretto, Tiepolo and Palma il Giovane. • Mon–Fri 9am–12.30pm • Campiello della Scuola 2454

Santa Maria Gloriosa dei Frari (D4) The Franciscan church is the city's largest, after St Mark's basilica, and its bell tower at 80 m (262 ft) is one of the tallest. Inside the church is a unique group of 124 wooden stalls carved by Marco Cozzi in the 15th century. Its best-known work of art is Titian's *Assumption* at the end of the central apse, but there are many others, including a mar-

CARNIVAL MASKS

Few visitors to Venice can resist buying a souvenir mask or two; in any case they are rather difficult to avoid! The craftsmen are artists in their own right, for besides having to master the basic techniques of mask-making, they need a lot of imagination and skill to create something unique. First, the clay model is fashioned to form the shape of the mask. This is covered in plaster, which hardens to make a mould. The actual mask is then built up with papier-mâché.

The glue dries to a smooth, shiny finish that resembles porcelain. After polishing, a white varnish is applied, then holes are punched out for the

eyes and the facial features are painted in. During Carnival time on the Piazzetta dei Leoni, some people have masks painted directly onto their faces.

ble statue of John the Baptist by Sansovino, a wooden statue of the same saint by Donatello, and a triptych of the Madonna and Child by Giovanni Bellini. Above the Pesaro altar is a splendid retable by Titian. The tomb of Monteverdi can be seen in the chapel next to the baptismal font. Titian is also honoured by a 19th-century monument, but his exact place of burial remains unknown. • Campo dei Frari

Casa Goldoni (D4) The former home of Carlo Goldoni, the celebrated 18th-century dramatist, now houses a museum and library devoted to the theatre and *commedia dell'arte*. The inner courtyard is an especially attractive example of 15th-century domestic architecture. • **Daily (except Sun) 10am– 5pm; winter months 10am–4pm. Last entry one hour before closing • San Tomà**

San Polo (D4) Overlooking one of the city's largest squares, where bull-baiting used to take place during Carnival, this church was originally a Byzantine construction but was altered in the 14th and 15th centuries. Inside, you can admire paintings by Tintoretto, Palma il Giovane, Veronese and Tiepolo. Flanking the entrance to the bell tower, opposite the church, are two lions, one holding a snake in its claws, the other toying with a man's head. • Campo San Polo

Palazzo Albrizzi (D4) Somewhat off the beaten track, this palace belonged to a family from Bergamo – a Venetian city on the mainland – that made its fortune trading in oil. They bought it floor by floor over 40 years. It is worth making the effort to visit the palace, to see its interior, richly decorated in gold and white stucco. • **Visits on request** ☎ 041 523 25 44 • Campiello Albrizzi

Ponte delle Tette (D3) In the part of town known as delle Carampane, the "Nipples Bridge" over the Rio di San Cassiano used to be a place of ill repute. Crossing over the bridge, prospective clients could ogle at the prostitutes flaunting their charms from the windows of the houses opposite. This entire area was given over to brothels, encouraged by the Venetian authorities who hoped they would contain the widespread practice of homosexuality.

Rialto Markets (E3) Venice flourished as a commercial city through trade with the Orient. Cargoes of exotic goods were unloaded at the markets near

A harmony of faded colours in a quiet backwater.

the Rialto and by the Grand Canal. Even today, these markets are a hive of activity; they are open every morning; by midday everything has been cleared away and the cats slink in to finish up the leftovers. The surrounding streets are full of budget-price shops and boutiques. Flowers, fruit and vegetables are on sale at the **Erberia**; there are a few stalls proposing clothing and souvenirs. On **Campo della Pescheria**, the covered fish market with its live crab and lobster and slippery eels is a sight not to be missed – it has been held there for 1,000 years. All kind of wares can be found at the bustling and picturesque market held on **Campo delle Beccarie** on the site of the old slaughterhouses, surrounded by the typical Venetian bistros called *bacari*.

San Giacomo di Rialto (E4) This little church is said to be the city's oldest (5th century). It still has its original interior marble columns and capitals, but the façade was added in the 14th century and altered several times since then.
• Campo San Giacomo di Rialto

WALKING TOUR: SAN POLO

From vaporetto station walk inland to **Campo San Tomà**. At the far end, the façade of the old **Scuola dei Calegheri**, Cobblers' Confraternity (no. 2857) has a marble relief of St Mark curing their patron saint, Aniano. Left of the church of San Tomà, Calle del Traghetto leads to Campiello San Tomà and over a bridge to **Casa Goldoni**, the playwright's home and museum in the 15th-century Gothic Palazzo Centani (no. 2795) with a picturesque inner courtyard. From Calle Tomà, cross Rio Terrà di Nomboli to turn right on Calle Saoneri, noting for later the traditional Osteria Al Ponte La Patatina, just before crossing the bridge into **Campo San Polo**. This centre of the sestiere's lively neighbourhood life stages open-air cinema in summer. The largest square after San Marco, it is surrounded by the originally Byzantine **Chiesa San Polo** and several fine *palazzi*, including 15th-century **Maffetti-Tiepolo** (no. 1957), **Corner-Mocenigo** (no. 2128) and the Gothic **Soranzo** (no. 2171).

Leave the Campo by Calle Bernardo, past mullion-windowed 15th-century **Palazzo Bernardo** (no. 2195) and across a bridge to Calle di Scaleter. Turn left on Rio Terrà Secondo to Calle della Chiesa. At the canal, fork right over a bridge to Calle Vida, past the Palazzo Giustinian, then, over to the right, Longhena's 17th-century **Palazzo Zane-Collalto**. Zigzag right and left to the lovely Renaissance Campiello (courtyard) of **Scuola Grande di San Giovanni Evangelista** and the adjacent church. Follow the signs from Calle Magazen round to the lofty late Gothic Franciscan church of **Santa Maria Gloriosa dei Frari**, once known as the "Ca' Grande", famous for its masterpieces by Titian, Bellini and Donatello. Behind the church is the **Scuola Grande di San Rocco**, where a confraternity of *battuti* (flagellants) commissioned Tintoretto's works tracing the life of Montpellier-born Saint Roch as healer of the sick.

On your way back to the San Tomà vaporetto station, stop off at the boutique of **Michele Cigogna**, Campo San Tomà 2867, renowned antique-restorer whose exquisitely painted wooden boxes make charming, if expensive gifts.

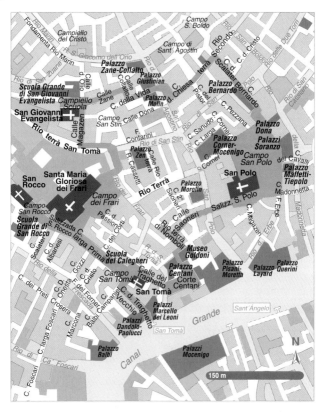

The sestiere celebrates in its palazzi and churches some of Venice's greatest artists, from playwright Carlo Goldoni to painters Bellini, Titian and Tintoretto.

Start: Vaporetto San Tomà

Finish: Vaporetto San Tomà

VENICE FOR CHILDREN

Most children are drawn to the town's own unique magic, the sheer fantasy land to be discovered wandering along little canals, up and down humpback bridges and ducking around blind alleys. Just walking around town can seem like a perpetual game of hide-and-seek.

Boats Galore

Children can get their first experience of a gondola on the low-fare *traghetti* ferry-rides across the Grand Canal. Boat-spotting is a popular sport, the Top Ten being the *Vaporetto* water bus; faster, streamlined *Motoscafo* motor launch; big *Motonave* ferry-boats for trips to the islands and the Lido; *Bragozzo* fishing boats in the lagoon, especially around Chioggia; garbage-collection boats; ambulance; fire-boats; police launches; black-draped, flower-bedecked funeral gondolas; and white-veiled wedding gondolas. See them being repaired in the venerable Squero di San Trovaso boatyard.

Sightseeing

Favourites with the kids are the view from the top of the Campanile on San Marco; the *Piombi* prison dungeons and torture chambers in the Palazzo Ducale; the model boats in the naval history museum (Campo San Biagio); glass-blowing on Murano and lace-making on Burano. If they bring along their roller blades, they can try them out on Campo Santa Margherita and Campo Santa Maria Formosa. There are great children's flea-markets on Campo del Ghetto and Campo San Polo (dates from the tourist office).

Goodies to Eat

The town's ice cream parlours, *gelaterie*, are almost as sacred as the Baroque churches, and as plentiful as the Gothic *palazzi*. Pastry shops, *pasticcerie*, come close behind in the popularity stakes. Sweet biscuits have fanciful names – ring-shaped *bussolai*, S-shaped *buranei*, chocolate and marzipan *basi di dama* (lady's kisses) and chocolate-iced *lingue di suocera* (mother-in-law's tongues). Other favourites are *spumiglie* meringues, crunchy almond and fennel-seed *sbreghette* and cornflour *zaleti* with raisins and pinenuts. Two Carnival specialities are *fritole* (sweet fritters) and crispy *crostoli*.

Toys

Carnival masks and costumed dolls are on sale all over town, but one of the most fascinating shops is La Scialuppa (Calle Seconda Saoneri, Dorsoduro 2681), specializing in historic model boats and kits to build a gondola.

Carnival and Other Festivals

With luck, Carnival time (two weeks before Lent) may coincide with school holidays, and visitors are invited to join in the fun of dressing up in fancy costumes and masks. Near San Marco, make-up artists gather on Piazzetta dei Leoncini to paint wonderful masks right on your face. For the Festival of Redentore on the third weekend of July, parties are held on a bridge of boats formed between the Zattere and Giudecca's Redentore church, culminating in a grand fireworks display. Most colourful of the events on the Grand Canal is the Historical Regatta on the first Sunday of September.

CANNAREGIO

For many, this is the living heart of Venice, a *sestiere* made up of small businesses and workshops, and one of the most populous. It takes up all of the northwestern sector of the city between the Grand Canal and the lagoon. In the middle is the Ghetto, an area surrounded by water where for three centuries all the Jews were forced to live.

THE DISTRICT AT A GLANCE

🏛 **SIGHTS**

Architecture
Santa Maria
di Nazareth
degli Scalzi 58

Ponte delle Guglie....58

San Giobbe 59

San Marcuola 59

Sant'Alvise 60

Madonna dell'Orto ..60

Santa Maria della
Misericordia 60

Gesuiti 61

San Giovanni
Crisostomo..............61

Art
Ca' d'Oro ★ 61

Atmosphere
Fondamenta Venier-
Savorgnan ★ 58

Campo della
Maddalena..............60

Fondamenta della
Sensa 60

Fondamenta Nuove..61

Corte del Milion.......61

Museums
Museo Comunità
Ebraica ★ 60

👫 **WALKING
TOUR   62**

☕ **WINING AND
DINING   80**

Santa Maria di Nazareth degli Scalzi (C3) Longhena designed this church (1654), for a community of Discalced (barefooted) Carmelites. The decoration is similar to Roman baroque; the façade is the only one in Venice to be made of Carrara marble. Inside are paintings by Tiepolo. • Fondamenta degli Scalzi

Ponte delle Guglie (C2) Just beyond the Palazzo Labia, the bridge with two obelisks at each end was built in 1580, in a single span. It leads to Rio Terrà San Leonardo, where a picturesque fish, fruit and vegetable market is held daily.

Fondamenta Venier-Savorgnan (C2) This quay borders the wide and luminous Cannaregio Canal. See the two splendid palaces, Palazzo Priuli-Manfrin,

Venice has more than 400 bridges, of wood, brick, stone and metal.

in neoclassical style, and the 17th-century Palazzo Savorgnan, with its spacious gardens open to the public.

San Giobbe (C2) Begun in 1450 in Gothic style and finished with Renaissance details, the church is famous for the sophisticated decoration of the portal and the interior vaulting. The Martini Chapel (second chapel on the left) is noteworthy for its vaulted ceiling of varnished polychrome terracotta tiles from the Florentine workshop of Luca della Robbia. • Campo San Giobbe

San Marcuola (D2) Dedicated to saints Ermagora and Fortunato, whose names are contracted into Marcuola in Venetian dialect, the church stands behind one of the rare *campi* opening directly onto the Grand Canal. It was founded at the beginning of the 11th century and rebuilt in the 12th and 18th centuries. The altars were sculpted by Morlaiter, and there's a splendid *Last Supper* by Tintoretto. • Campo San Marcuola

Museo Comunità Ebraica (D2) On the ground floor of a synagogue built in 1528, the museum displays examples of Venetian Jewish art dating from the 17th–19th centuries, tapestries and manuscripts. Note the height of the houses in the Ghetto – they were built with six to nine storeys to make up for lack of ground space. • Daily June–Sept (except Sat and Jewish holidays) 10am–7pm; Oct–May 10am–6pm. For guided tours of synagogues and Jewish cemeteries ☎ 041 71 53 59 • Schola Grande Tedesca Campo di Ghetto Nuovo 2902

Campo della Maddalena (D2) Behind the Palazzo Vendramin-Calergi, this quiet square is particularly beautiful, surrounded by simple houses topped with imposing chimneys.

Fondamenta della Sensa (D1) The long straight line of the Sensa Canal and its quays, buildings and gardens provide striking perspectives. Its southerly aspect, tranquillity and greenery have encouraged the construction of some handsome palaces.

Sant'Alvise (D1) The charm of this church of 1388 resides in the contrast between its rustic exterior and the sumptuous interior decoration, enhanced by Tiepolo paintings. • Campo Sant'Alvise

Madonna dell'Orto (E2) A 14th-century church rebuilt or altered in the 15th century, with statues of the Twelve Apostles in niches decorating its magnificent terracotta façade, the most complete purely Gothic façade in the city. First dedicated to St Christopher, it was reconsecrated to the Virgin after a 14th-century statue of her was found in a neighbouring garden. The interior, bathed in light from the upper windows, has three aisles, adorned with some of Tintoretto's most important work. He is buried with his son Domenico in the apse to the right of the choir. • Campo della Madonna dell'Orto

Santa Maria della Misericordia (Santa Maria Valverde) (E2) The church, with adjoining abbey, was built in the 10th century, and altered several times from the 13th century. Its pretty *campo*, with the original terracotta paving, retains all the charm of a bygone age. • Campo dell'Abbazia

Ca' d'Oro (E3) The 15th-century Gothic "Golden House", with a façade of marble tracery, takes its name from its once-gilded exterior. It houses the *Galleria Franchetti*, which extends into the neighbouring Palazzo Giusti. Displays include collections of Italian and foreign paintings, sculpture in marble and bronze, and ceramics. In addition to Mantegna's famous *Saint Sebastian*, there are significant works by Titian, Tintoretto, Van Eyck, Guardi and Giovanni Bellini. • Mon 8.15am–2pm; Tues–Sun 8.15am–7.15pm. Last entry one hour before closing • Calle Ca' d'Oro 3933

Fondamenta Nuove (E2–F3) This quay offers a magnificent view of San Michele and Murano, the nearest islands of the lagoon.

Gesuiti (Santa Maria Assunta) (F2) Built by the Jesuits (c.1730), the church in the form of a Latin cross and with a splendid baroque façade became first a school and then a barracks when the militant order was disbanded in 1773. The interior is embellished with important paintings by Titian and Tintoretto. • Campo dei Gesuiti

San Giovanni Crisostomo (E3) An elegant bell-tower dominates the simple Renaissance façade of this church rebuilt between 1497 and 1504. Most remarkable among its many works of art an outstanding late work by Giovanni Bellini, *St Jerome, St Christopher and St Augustine* (1513) at the first altar to the right. • Salizzada San Giovanni Crisostomo

Corte del Milion (E3) The area stretching behind the church of San Giovanni Crisostomo is called the Corte del Milion. Tradition has it that Marco Polo lived at no. 5845 until his death in 1324 – *Il Milione* was the title of the great traveller's memoirs from the Far East. Many of the neighbouring buildings have retained details from past eras, such as Byzantine friezes.

WALKING TOUR: CANNAREGIO

From the rich Baroque façade of the 17th-century **Chiesa degli Scalzi** ("Barefoot" Carmelites), follow the busy Rio Terrà Lista di Spagna shopping street to **Campo San Geremia** with its church and 18th-century **Palazzo Labia** (offices of RAI television) at the confluence of the Canale di Cannaregio and Grand Canal. Turn left at the 16th-century **Ponte delle Guglie** along Fondamenta Venier-Savorgnan. The entrance to **Parco Savorgnan** public gardens is beside the **Palazzo Priuli-Venier-Manfrin** (342). Back on the Fondamenta, continue along to house number 469 leading to the audacious modern **Quartiere Saffa** housing built in the 1980s using historic Venetian forms and colours – ochre, pink, russet, lemon and redbrick. At the bridge, turn left to 15th-century **Chiesa San Giobbe** (St Job), Venice's first Renaissance-style church. Double back and cross the **Ponte dei Tre Archi**, the town's only three-arched bridge then turn right, passing on your left the splendid 17th-century **Palazzo Surian-Bellotto** as you follow the canal to the open-air fish-stalls.

Turn left on **Calle Ghetto Vecchio** into the old Jewish Ghetto, hemmed in by its exceptionally tall 7- and 8-storey tenements. Of two 16th-century synagogues on the first square, **Schola Spagnola** (1654) and **La Levantina** (1635), the latter is open for Sabbath services. Continue across a bridge to the spacious **Campo Ghetto Nuovo**, surrounded by shops and three other synagogues, also 16th-century but incorporated in older buildings in the right-hand corner of the square: **Schola Italiana**, **Schola Tedesca** (German) housing the Museo Ebraico (2902), and **Schola Canton**, founded by Provençal refugees. Continue north across a bridge over the Rio della Misericordia to look back and take in what was originally the Ghetto's self-contained island. Calle della Malvasia leads across two other canals to the secluded, almost rustic **Campo Sant'Alvise** (Venetian dialect name for St Louis of Toulouse) with its 14th-century Gothic convent church close to the Lagoon.

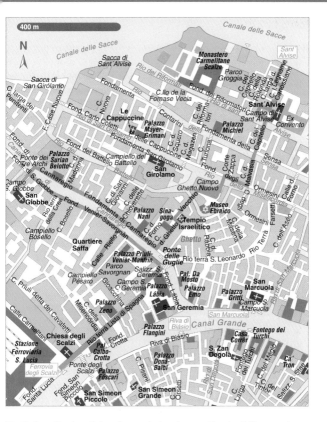

Stroll along the town's less frequented waterway, Canale di Cannaregio, and discover some unexpectedly attractive modern housing and the historic Ghetto.
Start: Vaporetto Ferrovia
Finish: Vaporetto Sant'Alvise

CASTELLO

This *sestiere* was probably named after a castle built here in Roman times. It is the most extensive of the districts of Venice, and owes much of its charm to its working-class atmosphere. The Arsenal, created in the 12th century, was crucial to the development of this part of town. At the far eastern edge of the urban area, Isola di San Pietro was the first of all the lagoon islands to be inhabited, possibly in the late 6th century.

THE DISTRICT AT A GLANCE

🏛 **SIGHTS**

Architecture
Santa Maria
dei Miracoli ★ 64

Santi Giovanni e
Paolo ★ 64

Santa Maria
Formosa ★ 65

San Zaccaria 65

Pietà 66

San Giovanni in
Bràgora 66

Scuola di San Giorgio
degli Schiavoni ★ 67

San Francesco della
Vigna 67

Art
Fondazione Querini-
Stampalia 65

Atmosphere
Salizzada San Lio 65

Riva degli
Schiavoni ★ 66

Campo delle Gorne ..67

Arsenale..................67

Museums
San Giorgio dei
Greci 66

Museo Storico
Navale 67

Greenery
Giardini Pubblici ★ 67

🚶 **WALKING TOUR**   68

☕ **WINING AND DINING**   81

Santa Maria dei Miracoli (F3) The small, isolated church is one of the earliest and most attractive examples of Venetian-Renaissance architecture, like a jewellery box inlaid with precious polychrome marble (said to be left over from the construction of San Marco). It was built to enshrine an image of the Virgin which had become an object of great veneration. • Campo dei Miracoli

Santi Giovanni e Paolo (F3) Popularly known as "San Zanipolo", this grand Dominican church is one of the greatest examples of Venetian-Gothic architecture. From the 15th century, the funerals of 25 doges were celebrated here; some fine monumental tombs, by Pietro Lombardo, can be seen along the west wall. Among the works of art, see the altar painting by Lorenzo Lotto, *Sant'Antonini Giving Alms*, on the rear wall of the transept and Veronese's *Annunciation, Asssumption and Adoration of the Shepherds* in the nearby Capella del Rosario. Proudly surveying the vast Campo's imposing Dominican monastery church and adjoining Scuola Grande di San Marco is Andrea Verrocchio's splendid equestrian statue (1488) of Bartolomeo Colleoni. After 21 years' loyal service, the *condottiere* willed his fortune to the Republic on the understanding that his statue would be on Piazza San Marco, but the Council compromised with a spot in front of the Scuola di San Marco. • **Campo dei Santi Giovanni e Paolo**

Salizzada San Lio (F4) In ancient times this was a busy commercial road; it has two interesting examples of 13th-century Byzantine tower-houses joined by an arch.

Santa Maria Formosa (F4) It is said that this church was raised in 639 by San Magno, a Friuli bishop. It was rebuilt in the shape of a Latin cross in the 15th century, and a century later the family of Admiral Vincenzo Cappello erected the main façade to honour his memory. Note the grimacing head above the entrance to the Baroque campanile. The *campo* is one of the largest in the city, site of a food and clothes market surrounded by palaces and lively cafés. • **Campo Santa Maria Formosa**

Fondazione Querini-Stampalia (F4) The second floor of the Querini-Stampalia palace holds a large collection of 14th–18th-century works of art, with paintings by Palma il Giovane, Luca Giordano and Giovanni Bellini. The façade of the palace (1528) gives onto a charming little *campiello* beside the Santa Maria Formosa canal and follows the curve of its banks. • **Daily (except Mon)** 10am–6pm; Fri, Sat 10am–10pm • **Castello 5252**

San Zaccaria (F5) The 12th-century Romanesque church was rebuilt in 1490 in Renaissance style. The interior is a charming blend of different styles. Of the church's many monumental canvases, the masterpiece is an altarpiece by Giovanni Bellini, *The Holy Conversation*. • **Campo San Zaccaria**

FAMOUS FOOTSTEPS

Peter Ilyich Tchaikovsky

(1840–93)
The composer wrote his Fourth Symphony at a hotel on the Riva degli Schiavoni in 1877. He dedicated it to Nadezda von Meck, a wealthy widow he never met and who repaid the honour with a monthly stipend and 13 years of platonic but, she said, insanely jealous love.

Riva degli Schiavoni (F–G5) Leading from Piazza San Marco to the public gardens, the long, lively quay is the perfect place to soak up the Venetian atmosphere. Its name comes from the Schiavonian or Slavonic (Dalmatian) seafarers who used to conduct their business here. Luxury hotels and palaces line the quay: the Palazzo delle Prigioni in Istrian stone, Palazzo Dandolo, which is now the renowned Danieli Hotel, and Palazzo Gabrielli, also a hotel.

Pietà (Santa Maria della Visitazione) (G5) Built 1745–60, the church has an elegant nave designed for concerts, a luminous Tiepolo painting on the ceiling and a vast entrance designed to eliminate outside noise. • Calle della Pietà

San Giovanni in Bràgora (G5) The primitive 8th-century church was rebuilt in the 9th century and consecrated to Saint John the Baptist when his relics were brought from the Orient. Today's building dates from the 16th century. The Gothic interior is adorned with works by Cima da Conegliano, Alvise Vivarini and Palma il Giovane. Vivaldi was baptised here in 1675. • Campo della Bràgora

San Giorgio dei Greci (G5) This dignified church, with its elegant bell tower, belonged to the Greek Orthodox community, the biggest foreign community in Renaissance Venice. The interior is richly decorated with Byzantine paintings and icons. The church houses the Museo dell'Istituto Ellenico di Studi Bizantini e Post-Bizantini, displaying icons and other sacred objects of the Greek Orthodox ritual. • Mon–Sat 9am–12.30pm and 2–4.30pm; Sun 9am–5pm • Ponte dei Greci 3412

Scuola di San Giorgio degli Schiavoni (G4) The Schiavoni confraternity founded this school in the 15th century. It displays paintings by Vittore Carpaccio (*Triumph of St George, Baptism of the Selenites*) and, on the first floor, a collection of other works from the mid-17th century. • Tues–Sat 10am– 12.30pm and 3–6pm; Sun 10am–12.30pm • Calle dei Furlani

San Francesco della Vigna (G4) The grandiose façade of this church was completed between 1564 and 1570 to a blueprint by Palladio. Inside there is an altarpiece (1562) by Veronese. The bell tower, similar to that of San Marco, is one of the tallest in the city. • Campo San Francesco della Vigna

Campo delle Gorne (G5) A canal runs along the *campo* and beyond it rises the wall of the Arsenal, decorated with great stone gargoyles *(gorne)* that keep watch over the low buildings of this quiet, working-class area.

Arsenale (G5) Out of bounds to tourists, the Arsenal is well protected by a rampart of high walls and a moat of natural and artificial canals. Inside is a vast complex of docks, factories and warehouses where the Venetian fleets were once built, the basis of the economic, political and military power of the glorious Republic. It is planned to install here a national naval museum to complement the Museo Storico Navale. • Campo dell'Arsenale

Museo Storico Navale (G5) The Naval Museum displays a model of the *Bucintoro*, the State galley of the doges destroyed by Napoleon's troops in 1798, and other Venetian vessels of the 18th century. • Mon–Fri (except public holidays) 8.45am–1.30pm; Sat 8.45am–1pm • Campo San Biagio 2148

Giardini Pubblici (H6) Napoleon had these gardens laid out on marshland, but the original design was modified in 1895 when the **Biennale Internazionale d'Arte** was introduced (held every odd-numbered year). Among the 18th-century statues, the *Monument to a Partisan,* in the lagoon, is the most poignant. From 1907, countries participating in the Biennale were invited to build their own pavilion; the result is a fascinating museum of modern architecture, notably for the designs of Austria's Josef Hoffmann, Finland's Alvar Aalto and Britain's James Stirling. • Riva dei Sette Martiri

WALKING TOUR: CASTELLO

Left of the Basilica San Marco, take Calle della Canonica, turn right on the canal to cross Ponte della Canonica to spend a moment in Venice's sole Romanesque cloister, **Chiostro di Sant'Apollonia**, perfect place to escape the San Marco crowds. It now houses a museum of sacred art (*Museo Diocesano d'Arte sacra*). Follow Rugheta Sant'Apollonia across Campo San Filippo and turn right past Calle delle Rasse's **18th-century apartment buildings** to the modern annex of the luxury **Hotel Danieli**, located principally out on the Riva degli Schiavoni in the 15th-century Gothic Palazzo Dandolfo, a favourite of Charles Dickens. On the Riva degli Schiavoni, cross the bridge and duck left through the Sottoportego San Zaccaria, yellow-signposted to the monumental Renaissance **Chiesa San Zaccaria**. Leave Campo San Zaccaria from the left on Calle San Provolo and right along the curving Fondamenta dell'Osmarin to cross Ponte del Diavolo on Campo San Severo to **Palazzo Priuli** with its Gothic-arched doorway (4999).

Turn left on Salizzada Zorzi past 15th-century **Palazzo Zorzi** and take a look at its courtyard (4930). Turn right on Ruga Giuffa and then to the left of **Chiesa Santa Maria Formosa** and Baroque campanile to the prettily located canalside **Palazzo Querini-Stampalia**, now a public library and art museum. Double back to **Campo Santa Maria Formosa**, always lively with its popular little market and cafés. At the rear of the Campo, by the Palazzo Riuli-Ruzzini (5866), cross the bridge to the Gothic cusped **Arco del Paradiso** with its statue of Madonna della Misericordia. Beyond the arch, **Calle del Paradiso** is lined with medieval shops and taverns separated from the overhanging upper floor by their original sturdy oak beams. Turn right on **Salizzada San Lio** (Leone), a busy but also medieval shopping street with 12th- and 13th-century Venetian-Byzantine palazzetti at 5691 and 5662 and the 17th-century **Chiesa San Lio** discreetly set back on a little Campo.

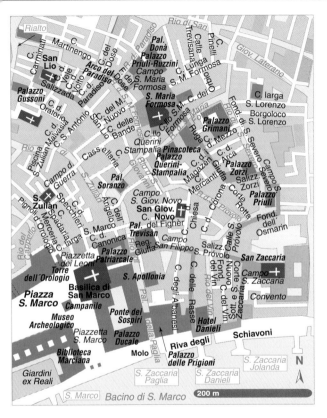

This walk delves into the medieval city from a Romanesque cloister via a promenade along Riva degli Schiavoni around to bustling Salizzada San Lio.

Start: Vaporetto San Marco

Finish: Vaporetto Rialto

THE ISLANDS

The Venice lagoon is a small inland sea more than 50 km (30 miles) long and 8–14 km (5–9 miles) wide, with a surface area of over 550 sq km (215 sq miles). Seeing the islands will help you understand more of Venice and its unique quality. Of the inhabited islands, the biggest are La Giudecca, San Giorgio Maggiore, Lido, Murano, Burano and Torcello.

LA GIUDECCA

A long, thin island, La Giudecca is just a stone's throw from Dorsoduro. Three quays – Fondamenta della Croce, delle Zitelle and di San Giovanni – line the Canale della Giudecca. At the western end there are several small 15th-century palaces and an incongruous neo-Gothic structure called the Mulino Stucky, a flour mill built in 1896 by a Swiss industrialist. He was assassinated by one of his employees in 1910 and the mill was finally closed down in the 1950s. After years of abandon, it is being renovated into shops, convention centre and apartments. • Two minutes from the Zattere by vaporetto line 82

Il Redentore The impressive terracotta-coloured Church of the Redeemer was built at the end of the 16th century, in response to a vow made when the plague was ravaging the city. In 1577, when the number of victims declined, Andrea Palladio was commissioned to begin the work. It was completed by Antonio da Ponte in 1592. During the Redentore festival in July, the church is linked to the Santa Maria della Salute basilica, opposite, by a bridge of boats. The church contains a fine *Baptism of Christ* by Veronese, as well as canvases by Tintoretto and Palma il Giovane. • Fondamenta San Giacomo

Sant'Eufemia Built in the 9th century, the church has been altered several times, with wall and ceiling paintings by 19-year-old Giambattista Canal, in 1764. In the left aisle, see the marble *Pietà* by Morlaiter. • Fondamenta Sant'Eufemia

SAN GIORGIO MAGGIORE

Lying off the eastern tip of La Giudecca, this island is taken up almost entirely by a Benedictine monastery. The church was designed by Andrea Palladio, begun in 1566 but completed after his death. Apart from paintings by Sebastiano Ricci and Jacopo Bassano, see in the choir two works by Tintoretto, and in the Conclave room, to the right of the choir, a retable by Carpaccio depicting St George slaying the dragon. The monastery is now the headquarters of the Cini Foundation; it has a permanent collection of paintings, furniture and antiques and organizes temporary art exhibitions. There's an open-air theatre in the gardens, the Teatro Verde. • **Vaporetto line 82 from the Zitelle landing-stage on La Giudecca**

LIDO

Sheltering the lagoon from the sea, the Lido is a long spit of sand, 12 km (7 miles) long and 4 km (just over 2 miles) wide. Even though its 19th-century romantic charm has now faded, many people find it pleasant to stroll along the promenade by the sea (Lungomare Guglielmo Marconi) and admire the famous Grand Hotel des Bains (which featured in the film *Death in Venice*), the casino, the Mostra palace where the Venice Film Festival is held, and the Grand Hotel Excelsior. Rent a bicycle or tandem at the intersection of Gran Viale and Via Zara and pedal off to explore the rest of the island. In the south is the small Malamocco quarter, founded in the 14th century, where you can see the Palazzo del Podestà and the Santa Maria Assunta church. The beach and the dunes at Alberoni, a small resort at the southern tip of the Lido, are worth seeing. South again is the small island of Pellestrina, with its fishing villages and *murazzi*, sturdy sea walls to contain the fury of the waves. Extensive work is being undertaken here to combat the flooding of the Lagoon's islands and Venice itself. • **Direct service**

FAMOUS FOOTSTEPS

Thomas Mann

(1875–1955)
It was in May 1911 at the Lido's Grand Hôtel des Bains that the great German novelist witnessed the disturbing elements for his short story, *Death in Venice*: the crooked gondolier, lecherous singer, above all, the beautiful Polish youth who enchanted him on the beach. All this amid "the flattering and suspect beauty of a town half fairytale, half trap for strangers."

by vaporetto line 6 from the Riva degli Schiavoni (6 minute crossing). Lines 1 (frequent stops, journey time about one hour), 51, 52 and 82 (the latter only in summer) also call at the Lido. If you are in a car, ferry 17 (automezzi) from Tronchetto (crossing time 35 minutes).

San Nicolò In the northeast corner of the island, the Benedictine church and monastery were founded in the first half of the 11th century. It was in this church that Mass was celebrated after the ceremony of the wedding of Venice to the sea. Every year for 800 years, until the abolition of the Republic by Napoleon, the Doge of Venice set out from the Lido towards the open sea on board the magnificent galley *Bucintoro*, followed by the gondolas of the other leading citizens. There he threw a ring into the waters, declaiming "We wed ourselves to you, our sea, as a sign of true and perpetual domination". This splendid ceremony has now been revived as a tourist attraction, with the Mayor tossing the ring into the sea.

Antico Cimitero Israelitico Alongside San Nicolò, the Jewish cemetery is one of the oldest in Europe, consecrated in 1389. The monumental tombs date from the 16th and 17th centuries.

San Lazzaro degli Armeni Anchored a short distance to the west of the Lido, this small island became the home of the Mechitar Fathers of the Roman Catholic Armenian Church in 1717. In the midst of a lovely garden of rare flowers and plants, the monastery includes a library with a precious collection of more than 2,000 Armenian illuminated manuscripts, a museum, an art gallery and an 18th-century printing house. One room of the museum is devoted to Lord Byron, who liked to come here to find peace of mind.

MURANO
The city of Venice sent all its glass-blowers to Murano in 1291 for security reasons – the Venetian houses were built of wood. In the 13th century the island had 30,000 residents, with its own government and aristocracy, and minted its own money. By the 15th century it was the most important centre of glass production in Europe. The craftsmen enjoyed unprecedented privileges, but in order to safeguard their special, highly secret techniques, they were forbidden to leave

A windowbox of hardy perennials to suit any climate.

Murano to work elsewhere. • **Vaporetti lines 41, 42, LN. Direct service during the tourist season from Fondamenta Nuove (crossing time 7 minutes).**

Museo del Vetro Before you fall into the clutches of the glass-vendors, call into the museum and learn to distinguish your *murrine millefiori* from your *cabochons*. Housed in the Palazzo Giustinian, the museum contains a collection of superb glassware from the 2nd century BC to the 2nd century AD and from the 15th century to the present. • **Daily (except Wed) 10am–4pm • Fondamenta Giustinian 8**

Basilica dei Santi Maria e Donato As your boat approaches the island you will admire the arcaded apse and bell tower of the red-brick basilica, mirrored in the water. Founded in the 7th century and rebuilt in the 12th, the church is one of the best examples of Venetian-Byzantine architecture. Its marble mosaic paving is extraordinary, a complex design depicting animals, insects and birds.

In the apse, see the serene blue *Praying Madonna* on a golden background. •
Fondamenta Giustinian

San Pietro Martire Behind its Renaissance colonnade, this church houses the
splendid Barbarigo altarpiece by Giovanni Bellini (1488). • **Fondamenta da
Mula**

BURANO

Fishing was at one time the
principal activity of the Bu-ra-
nelli (the inhabitants of Burano), who painted their houses
in startlingly bright and con-
trasting colours so they could
recognize them from far out
at sea. The women were
famed for their lacemaking, a
craft which developed on the
island at the beginning of the

16th century. Today you will still see groups of ladies sitting in the sun outside
their front doors, needle and white thread in hand and cushion on knee.
• Vaporetti lines LN, T from Fondamenta Nuove (crossing time about 40 minutes).

Museo del Merletto If you intend to buy lace on the island, visit the museum first, to acquire an eye for the real thing. Be aware that many of the offer-
ings fluttering from Burano's souvenir shop windows may well have been made
in China. The museum, run by a cooperative of women intent on protecting the
quality of their work, also includes a school and workshop. Exhibits cover three
centuries of lace-making, but only the 20th-century models were made in Burano itself. • **Daily (except Tues) 10am–4pm** • **Piazza Galuppi 187**

San Martino The church was built in the 16th century when the parish was
founded, and its lofty bell tower was added a century later. Inside you can see
an exceptional *Crucifixion* by Tiepolo. • **Piazza Baldassarre Galuppi**

TORCELLO

The large and wealthy settlement of 10,000 inhabitants that occupied Torcello from the 5th to 10th centuries has dwindled to a community of 60, living in a few houses scattered along a single pathway and clustered in the historic centre. Now much of the island is marshy and green and may get crowded as a very popular excusion for venetians at the weekend. Historically most significant are the cathedral, Santa Maria Assunta, the church of Santa Fosca, and an old marble throne called the Sedia di Attila, who visited the Lagoon with his Huns around 450, but probably did not sit there. It was also a favourite hangout of that other rowdy, Ernest Hemingway. • Vaporetti lines LN, T from Fondamenta Nuove (crossing time about 45 minutes).

Cattedrale di Santa Maria Assunta Said to date from 639, according to an inscription in the choir, the cathedral was rebuilt from the 9th to 11th centuries. The bell tower is one of the tallest of the lagoon. The cathedral is adorned with stunning Venetian-Byzantine mosaics, including a huge *Last Judgement* on the back of the façade, and a luminous *Madonna and Child* in the apse. Note also the mosaic paving and the magnificent iconostasis in lace-like marble sculpted with heraldic animals.

Santa Fosca Linked to the cathedral by the narthex, this elegant Romanesque church in the form of a Greek cross was built in 1100. On the altar is a 15th-century sculpture of Saint Fosca.

FAMOUS FOOTSTEPS

Ernest Hemingway
(1899–1961)
The rough tough macho man of American letters came to Venice in 1948 to drink at Harry's Bar and write his novel *Across the River and Into the Trees* on the island of Torcello. And go out shooting with the hotel gardener in the Lagoon. "I shot good," he told the *New Yorker*, "and thus became a respected local character."

Speek
Gorgonzola
e Carnia

Crudo di
Parma

Salame
Nostrano

cityBites

Our selection covers mainly medium-priced restaurants, where you can eat well at a reasonable cost, in the range of €20 to 30. If you want a snack or a less formal atmosphere, choose a *bacaro* (see p. 79). Prices vary from place to place and depend on whether you are at the bar, at an inside table, or on the terrace. For most of the year you can eat outdoors, enjoying the passing parade as much as your meal. Closing days may change suddenly, so it's always best to phone in advance.

Venice boasts some excellent local dishes but is best renowned for the superb seafood. There are plenty of *pizzerie*, and light meals, pastries and other desserts, and all types of drinks are served in cafés. The Veneto area produces a number of pleasant red and white wines. The best local reds re Valpolicello, Valpantena and Bardolina, all light and dry. The most famous white wine from the region is Soave.

As for coffee, if you find Italian espresso too strong for your taste, ask for a *caffè lungo* (with extra water) or a *cappuccino*.

SAN MARCO

Ai Assassini
Rio Terrà dei
Assassini 3695
☎ 041 528 79 86
Closed Sat lunch
and Sun
Reservation advised.
Typical *bacaro* with a
simple menu of salads
and grilled meats
accompanied by good
wines.

Ai Mercanti
Corte Coppo 4346/A
☎ 041 523 82 69
Closed Sun,
Mon morning
Excellent fish restaurant,
sophisticated seafood
recipes.

Al Chianti
Calle Larga S. Marco 655
☎ 041 522 43 85
Closed Sun
Seafood spaghetti and
typical local specialities.

Al Conte Pescaor
Piscina San Zulian 597/A
☎ 041 522 14 83
Closed Sun
Wonderful fish dishes to
be enjoyed in a typical
Venetian atmosphere.

Al Volto
Calle Cavalli 4081
☎ 041 522 89 45
Closed Sun

*Osteria-enoteca
San Marco*

A simple but tasty menu;
over 500 vintages on the
wine list.

Arturo
Calle degli Assassini
3656/A
☎ 041 528 69 74
Closed Sun
Reservation essential;
credit cards not
accepted.
Meat specialities, fresh
produce (good *misto di
verdure*, vegetable fritters).
Venetian clientele.

Caffè Florian
Piazza San Marco 56/59
☎ 041 520 56 41
Closed Wed in winter
Famous throughout
Europe since 1720, this
grand café is enjoying a
revival. The coffee is
always fantastic.

Da Raffaele
Fondamenta delle
Ostreghe 2347
☎ 041 523 23 17
Closed Thurs
Fish a speciality, fresh and
well prepared.

Gran Caffè
Ristorante Quadri
Piazza San Marco 121
☎ 041 528 92 99
A 19th-century
establishment with a
small restaurant,
historically a rival to the
Caffè Florian. Both claim
to have introduced Turkish
coffee to Venice.

Le Bistrot de Venise
Calle dei Fabbri 4685
☎ 041 523 66 51
Closed Tues
Restaurant with typical
Venetian dishes, where
you can feast your ears on
music and your eyes on
an art exhibition while
you give your tastebuds a
treat.

Osteria al Bacareto
Calle Crosera 3447
☎ 041 528 93 36
Closed Sat evening and
Sun
Traditional dishes such as
bigoli in salsa (handmade
spaghetti), sarde in saor
(sardines in vinegar) and
liver with polenta.

Osteria alle Botteghe
Calle delle
Botteghe 3454
☎ Tel. 041 522 81 81
Closed Sun
Toast with cheese, and
porchetta (roast suckling
pig) sandwiches.

Osteria-enoteca
San Marco
San Marco 1610
Frezzeria
☎ 041 528 52 42
Closed Sun
Run by four young people,
this restored restaurant-
cum-wine bar is well
worth seeking out. The
imaginative use of herbs
transforms traditional
dishes. Good wine list.

DORSODURO

Da Codroma
Ponte del Soccorso
Fondamenta Briati 2540
☎ 041 524 67 89
Closed Sun, Mon
evening
Friendly *bacaro* serving
good wine and *cichetti*
until 1am, live jazz.

La Furatola
Calle Longa San Barnaba
2869/A
☎ 041 520 85 94
Closed Mon lunch, Thurs
A long-established
restaurant serving very
high-quality dishes.

Locanda Montin
Fondamenta
di Borgo 1147
☎ 041 522 71 51
Closed Wed in winter
A favourite with the
artistic community.
Venetian cuisine.

La Zucca

SANTA CROCE

Antica Besseta
Salizzada de
Ca' Zusto 1395
☎ 041 721 687
Closed Tues, and Wed
lunch in winter.
Book ahead.
A well-frequented small
restaurant. The traditional
Venetian risottos are
excellent, as are all the
fish specialities.

Alla Zucca
Ramo del Megio 1762
☎ 041 524 15 70
Closed Sun
A wide choice of
vegetarian dishes with
lots of vegetables, but
also soups, pasta, meat
dishes and couscous. A
few tables outside on the
terrace, near the bridge.

Ribò
Fondamenta Minotto 158
☎ 041 524 24 86
Closed Wed
Smart and discreet,
high-quality cuisine,
mostly fish but some meat
dishes. Indoor garden.

BACARI

Perhaps named in
honour of Bacchus, or
of the *bacara*, a wine-
jug in the local dialect,
the *bacaro* is a Venetian
institution– in custom if
not in décor and the
menu, not unlike an old
English pub. People
tend to congregate in
these bars just before
lunch or dinner, to meet
up with friends and
sample *cichetti*, savoury
dishes such as *baccalà*
cod, mortadella
sausage, *pancetta* raw
ham with bread, and so
on, helped along with
an *ombra* (a glass) of
wine, or two. This may
develop into a *giro di
ombre* – a "bacaro
crawl", going from one
to the other, snacking
and drinking until
closing time (around
9pm). Normally you eat
standing up, though
some of them do have a
few tables.

SAN POLO

Alla Madonna
Calle della Madonna 594
☎ 041 522 38 24
Closed Wed
At the end of the Rialto bridge, a well-known restaurant that's always packed with Venetians and tourists.

Antico Dolo
Ruga Vecchia
San Giovanni 778
☎ 041 522 65 46
The menu of this venerable establishment provides a wide choice of pasta and rice dishes, as well as *baccalà* (salt cod).

Cantina do Mori
Calle do Mori 401
☎ 041 522 54 01
Closed Sun
One of the oldest and most famous *bacari* in town, said to go back to the 15th century. There is an incredible choice of wines, and a variety of savoury *cichetti* to be sampled while you stand.

Cantina do Spade
Sottoportego
do Spade 860
☎ 041 521 05 74
Closed Sun in winter
Established in 1475: Casanova himself came here. If you can find an empty table, sit down and make your choice among the delicious pasta and rice dishes, fish sandwiches and *cichetti* based on game.

Due Colonne
Campo Sant'Agostin 2343
☎ 041 524 06 85
Closed Sun
Wide choice of pizzas to eat inside or take away.

Osteria Enoteca Vivaldi
Calle della
Madonnetta 1457
☎ 041 523 81 85
Closed Wed
Typical Venetian dishes. If you're not feeling very hungry, you can call in just for a glass of wine.

Poste Vecie
Rialto, Pescheria 1608
☎ 041 721 822
Closed Tues
Good restaurant with a pleasant terrace (open in the warm season) shaded by a pergola. Delicious fish risottos.

Vini da Pinto
Campo le Becarie 367
☎ 041 522 45 99
Closed Mon
Venerable *bacaro*, over 100 years old. It serves cooked sausages, *baccalà* (salt cod) and excellent wines.

Alla Palazzina

CANNAREGIO

A la Vecia Cavana
Rio Terrà SS. Apostoli 4624
☎ 041 528 71 06
A well-known restaurant specializing in fish dishes.

Al Milion
Corte Prima del
Milion 5841
☎ 041 522 93 02
Closed Wed
Typical Venetian dishes, such as chopped liver cooked in wine, or cuttlefish, in Marco Polo's house.

Al Vagon
Sottoportego del
Magazen 5597
☎ 041 523 75 58
Closed Tues
Excellent fish to be enjoyed on a charming terrace.

Alla Maddalena
Rio Terrà della
Maddalena 2348
☎ 041 720 723
Evenings only, 7–9pm
Closed Sun

Traditional sandwiches, *pasta e fasoi* (pasta with beans).

Alla Palazzina
Rio Terrà San Leonardo 1509
☎ 041 717 725
Closed Wed
A former *bacaro* converted into an elegant trattoria with a pergola on the Ponte delle Guglie.

Antica Mola
Fondamenta degli Ormesini 2800
☎ 041 717 492
Closed Wed
A popular trattoria in the Ghetto neighbourhood. Garden and waterside terrace.

Antico Gatoleto
Campo Santa Maria Nuova 6055
☎ 041 522 18 83
Inventive dishes by an imaginative chef, mostly based on fish. Pizzas served at lunchtime and in the evening.

Da Alvise
Fondamenta Nuove 5045
☎ 041 520 41 85
Closed Mon
Pizzeria-trattoria with a big terrace looking over the lagoon. Fresh seasonal produce, good selection of wines and beers.

Dal Mas
Lista di Spagna 150/A
Closed Tues
For a great start to your day, come to this bakery for a standing breakfast. You won't regret it!

Osteria Ca' d'Oro alla Vedova
Ramo Ca' d'Oro 3912
☎ 041 528 53 24
Closed Thurs and Sun morning
A well-restored historic *bacaro*, where you would be well advised to sample the delicious vegetable fritters *(misto di verdure)* or, in the evening, the starters.

Vini da Gigio
Fondamenta San Felice 3628/A
☎ 041 528 51 40
Closed Mon and Tues
A lively family-run restaurant buzzing with atmosphere and frequented by locals. Three- or four- course menus based on meat or fish, good choice of wines, and a great view.

CASTELLO

Al Giardinetto
Salizzada Zorzi 4928
☎ 041 528 53 32
Closed Thurs
In the Palazzo Zorzi, dating from 1400, this is a typical trattoria with pergola where you can eat outside in fine weather.

Alle Tastiere
Calle del Mondo Novo 5801
☎ 041 522 72 20
Closed Sun
Traditional dishes together with a few original culinary creations. Fish specialities.

Corte Sconta
Calle del Pestrin 3886
☎ 041 522 70 24
Closed Sun and Mon in Jan and 15 July–15 Aug
Reservation advised

An old, tastefully restored bistrot. The menu is restricted to fish, but the quality is equal to that of many more refined restaurants.

Didovich
Campo Santa Marina 5909
☎ 041 520 92 68
Closed Sun
Perfect if you just want coffee and a cake, this is an extraordinary pastry shop where everything is home-made. The favourite haunt of Donna Leon and her Commissario Guido Brunetti.

Hostaria da Franz
Fondamenta San Isepo 754
Corte del Magazen
☎ 041 522 08 61
Closed Tues and all Jan
Exceptional seafood spaghetti and for dessert, a *tiramisù* to die for. During the week open for dinner only, but on Saturday and Sunday lunch is also served.

Trattoria alla Rivetta
Ponte di San Provolo 4625
☎ 041 528 73 02
An unpretentious bistrot that is always packed. Try the traditional Venetian-style liver, and the black squid cooked in their ink.

THE ISLANDS

Altanella
Calle delle Erbe 268
La Giudecca
☎ 041 522 77 80
Closed Mon and Tues
A typical trattoria with service on the terrace in summer. A classical Venetian menu.

Harry's Dolci
Fondamenta San Biagio 773
La Giudecca
☎ 041 522 48 44
Closed Tues
Salads and cold food and dazzling desserts like lemon meringue or chocolate tart – luxury at everyday prices. In summer, sip a cocktail on the terrace with a view of the San Marco Canal. Just the place for a romantic escapade!

All'Artigliere
Via Sandro Gallo 83
Zona 4 Fontane
Lido
☎ 041 526 54 80
Closed Wed
Friendly welcome; excellent traditional cuisine. Try the *spaghetti all'artigliera* (with shellfish).

Trattoria Favorita
Via F. Duodo 33, Lido
☎ 041 52 616 26
Closed Mon and Tues lunch
Famous for grilled fish – *alla griglia* – and typical Venetian pasta dishes.

Trattoria ai Frati
Fondamenta Venier 4, Murano
☎ 041 736 694
Closed Thurs
Fish a speciality, and excellent home-made cakes.

Trattoria Busa alla Torre
Campo Santo Stefano 3 Murano
☎ 041 739 662
Daily 11.30am–4pm
Good food, pleasant atmosphere.

Al Gatto Nero
Fondamenta Giudecca 88, Burano
☎ 041 730 120
Closed Mon
Delicious *risotto alla buranella* and *pasticcio di pesce* (fish pie).

Locanda Cipriani
Piazza Santa Fosca 29 Torcello
☎ 041 730 150
Closed Tues and all winter.
Renowned elegant and charming restaurant, tranquil setting, sophisticated cuisine.

RISI E BISI

The name "rice and peas" sounds like nothing at all. In fact, this simple but savoury age-old Venetian risotto was ceremonially served every year to the Doge on the feast day of the city's patron saint Mark, April 25. And tradition required that the dear old Doge eat every last pea and grain of rice.

Be sure to use round and not long-grained rice. These days the first-class quality of frozen peas makes it a year-round dish, done up with chopped ham, grated cheese and parsley. Snooty Milanese and Genoese may contest the right of *risi e bisi* to be considered a real risotto, but such quibbles are beneath a Venetian's considerable dignity. A dry white wine is often added to the cooking, but it is best served with a light red wine from the Veneto region, a Valpolicella or sharper Bardolino.

Risi e Bisi for four
250 g peas (fresh or frozen)
250 g round-grain rice (Carnaroli)
70 g butter
1 litre heated chicken broth
$1/2$ cup dry white wine
50 g *pancetta*, diced
1 medium onion chopped
1 sprig of chopped parsley, salt, pepper, grated Parmesan cheese

Sauté the onions and pancetta with half the butter in the risotto pan and add the peas.
Add the wine and bring to a boil till almost evaporated.
Blend in the rice over moderate heat and cook gradually with chicken broth, adding a ladle at a time, stirring constantly, until completely cooked to a creamy texture.
Remove the pan from the heat and stir in most of the chopped parsley, add salt and pepper to taste, let the rest of the butter melt in, incorporate grated Parmesan.
Let stand 2 minutes and serve, decorated with rest of parsley.

CityNights

There are countless things to do during the day, but Venice has little to offer the night-owl by way of entertainment. As darkness falls, the city settles down to sleep; even in summer it is difficult to find anything open after midnight. The principal nocturnal pastime is a stroll through the deserted streets. If you fancy something more exciting, try one of the following bars, discotheques or theatres, or have a flutter at the casino.

BARS AND PIANO BARS

Al Theatro
Campo San Fantin 1916
San Marco
Daily (except Mon, off-season) 7.30am–2am
A very popular bar-restaurant with a pleasant terrace.

Bacaro Jazz
San Marco 5546
Daily (except Wed)
noon–midnight
Happy hours 2–7.30pm
A small establishment frequented by trend-setters, intellectuals and insomniacs.

Florian
Piazza San Marco
Daily (except Wed in winter)
7.30am–midnight
Select Venetian bar. In its 18th-century rooms (with live orchestra), relax and enjoy a cup of tea and snack, or something stronger.

Haig's Bar
Campo Santa Maria del Giglio 2477, San Marco
Daily (except Wed)
10am–2am
Quiet and not too expensive.

Harry's Bar
Calle Vallaresso 1323
San Marco
Daily (except Mon in winter) 10.30am–11pm
Splash out and soak up the atmosphere while sipping a "Bellini" cocktail in this bar, once the haunt of Hemingway and now a favourite of actors, writers and politicians.

Martini Scala Club
Campiello San Gaetano 1980, San Marco
Every evening (except Tues, and all July and August) 10pm–3.30am
Close to La Fenice theatre, this select piano bar is both live music bar and restaurant.

Ai Postali
Fondamenta Rio Marin 821, Santa Croce
Every evening (except Sun) 5pm–2am
Small bar with a youngish clientèle.

Café Blue
Calle Lunga San Pantalon 3778, Dorsoduro
Every evening (except Sun) 5pm–2am
Happy hour 8.30–9.30pm
Underground atmosphere.

Corner Pub
Calle della Chiesa 684
Dorsoduro
Daily (except Mon)
8pm–1am
Small pub, frequented by Brits and other English-speakers.

Il Caffè – Caffè Rosso
Campo Santa Margherita
Dorsoduro 2963
Every evening (except Sun) 7pm–1am
A trendy venue with bright red façade, the favourite haunt of

Caffè Florian

avant-garde students, musicians and arty types. Late night jazz.

Do Leoni
Riva degli Schiavoni 4176, Castello
A piano bar for lovers of good music

DISCOTHEQUES

Piccolo Mondo American Bar
Calle Corfu 1056/A, Dorsoduro
☎ 041 520 03 71
Every evening (except Mon) 10pm–4am

Bar 10am–6 or 10pm
Compulsory booking
A small place, always packed with revellers.

Acropolis
Lungomare Marconi 22 Lido
Daily in summer;
Sat only, end Sept–May
A pleasant disco overlooking the Lido beach.

THEATRES AND CONCERT HALLS

Gran Teatro La Fenice
San Marco 2847
☎ 041 786 511

Sala Concerti del Circolo Artistico
Palazzo delle Prigioni
San Marco
☎ 041 522 57 07

Teatro Fondamenta Nuove
Cannaregio 5013
☎ 041 522 44 98

Teatro Goldoni
Calle del Teatro o de la Comedia 4650/B
San Marco
☎ 041 240 20 11
This is the city's main live theatre venue.

Teatro Malibran
Campiello Malibran
Cannaregio
☎ 041 786 601

Teatro Toniolo
Piazzetta Cesare Battisti 1, Mestre
☎ 041 971 666

CASINO

The municipal Casino is at Lungomare Marconi 4, Lido, during the summer and at Palazzo Vendramin-Calergi, Cannaregio, in winter. The Casino is open every evening, and evening dress is required. If you don't want to tempt fate at the gambling tables, you can just have a drink and listen to the music in the nightclub.

CINEMA'S LOVE AFFAIR

For centuries, Venice seemed it was just waiting for the cinema to be invented. Visually, it provided the natural backdrop for wide-eyed romance, doomed love, grim treachery and tragic death, the staples of ten thousand screenplays to come. In August, 1896, barely eight months after presenting in Paris the world's first motion picture show, the Lumière brothers were in Venice filming the pigeons on Piazza San Marco and gondolas on the Grand Canal, for a standing-room-only show in the 17th-century Teatro Minerva on the Calle XXII Marzo.

Some ten years later, Mario Caserini directed here the first filmed version of *Othello*. Since then, there have been 12 films of Shakespeare's tragedy, three less than Venice's most popular film subject, *Casanova*, which provided Italy's first "talkie" in 1927. *Marco Polo* and *The Merchant of Venice* have garnered six apiece. Hollywood's first film shot in Venice, *The Italian* in 1914, the story of an Italian emigrant who began as a Venetian gondolier and ended up as a New York shoeshine boy.

Venice became the site of the world's first international film festival, as part of the Biennale in 1932. One good idea credited to the fascist regime of Mussolini, the Mostra del Cinema was at first open to all points of view, from capitalist Hollywood's Frank Capra to the Stalinist Soviet Union's Nikolai Ekk, with his prize-winning *Road to Life*. By 1938, it was dominated by fascist and Nazi propaganda. Since World War II, replacing the Coppa Mussolini with the Golden Lion, the Venice has rivalled Cannes' in attracting the world's most creative films.

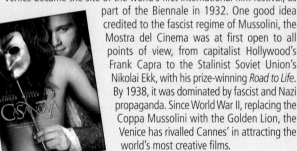

Certainly, the world's most celebrated directors have been seduced by this most photogenic of cities, from Max Reinhardt in 1913 to David Lean and Luchino Visconti in the modern era. The town's unique architecture, colour and light have drawn others like Joseph Mankiewicz to shoot his sophisticated comedy whodunnit, *The Honey Pot* (1967, with Rex Harrison and Susan Hayward) or Woody Allen for his pastiche musical, *Everyone Says "I Love You"* (1996). Not to forget obligatory speedboat chases for James Bond thrillers *From Russia with Love* and *Moonraker* (much to the distress of residents in their canalside *palazzi*).

More often, directors have been attracted by the melancholy darker side of Venice – Fritz Lang with *Der müde Tod* (Tired Death, 1921), Nicolas Roeg for his disturbing occult thriller *Don't Look Now* (1973, with Donald Sutherland and Julie Christie), and most memorably, Luchino Visconti directing Dirk Bogarde in *Death in Venice* (1970).

Visconti was happy to exploit the splendour of La Fenice opera house for his historic melodrama *Senso* (1954) about Venice's 1866 revolt against the Habsburg monarchy. For other directors, however, Venice's original beauty was not enough. Typically, the Grand Canal, on which Greta Garbo took a gondola ride for her 1935 version of *Anna Karenina*, was recreated in Hollywood, along with a "Chiesa della Salute" resembling a Turkish mosque. In his fantasy Venice for *Trouble in Paradise* (1932), Ernst Lubitsch had opera singer Enrico Caruso dub the gondolier's voice for *O Sole Mio*, a Neapolitan song. Rather than leave Rome for his *Casanova* in 1977, Fellini fashioned a lagoon and canals from vast sheets of black plastic spread out on the stages of the Cinecittà studio.

INTERNATIONAL FILM FESTIVAL

The Film Festival, founded in 1932, is held on the Lido each year at the end of August. Over the two weeks of the Festival, films are shown day and night in the Palace or Astra cinemas. Since it's virtually impossible to obtain tickets, you may have to be content with spotting the film stars enjoying a drink on the terrace of the Excelsior.

cityFacts

Airports	92
Banks	92
Climate	92
Currency and Exchange	92
Disabled Travellers	92
Driving	93
Electricity	93
Emergencies	93
Entry Regulations and Customs Allowance	93
Finding Your Way	94
Gondolas	94
Lost Property	95
Post Office	95
Public Holidays	95
Public Transport	96
Religious Services	96
Sightseeing Passes	96
Taxis	97
Telephone	97
Tides	98
Tipping	98
Tourist Offices	98
Water	98

Airports

The main airport is Venice Marco Polo, 13 km (8 miles) north of the city. Marco Polo is linked to the city by public bus, once an hour in winter and every half hour in summer. The journey takes about 20 minutes. Airport buses are slightly more expensive but are timed to coincide with arrivals and departures of major airlines. Both buses arrive at Piazzale Roma, from where you board the vaporetto, Line 1 making stops all along the Grand Canal. Line 82 takes a quicker route to San Marco.

Charter flights often use Treviso, 30 km (19 miles) to the north. To get to Venice you have to take bus No. 6 to the centre of Treviso then coach or train to Venice.

Banks

Venice's banks open 8.30am–1.30pm and 2.35–3.35pm, Monday to Friday. They close at 11.30am on local holidays and all day on national holidays and at weekends.

Climate

Venice can be damp, chilly and occasionally flooded from November to March, but the rest of the year it is pleasant, reaching a maximum of 28 °C (83 °F) in July and August.

Currency and Exchange

The Italian currency is the euro, divided into 100 cents or *centesimi*. Money can be changed at banks, at currency exchange offices *(cambio)* or your hotel. Exchange offices open weekdays 9am–12.30pm and 3–7.30pm; some open on Saturdays in the tourist season (the hours are posted in each office). The exchange office at Santa Lucia Station also opens on Sundays, 8.30am–7pm, and the one at Marco Polo Airport opens every day 9am–7.30pm.

Disabled Travellers

Venice is not an easy city to negotiate in a wheelchair, as most of the bridges have steps at each end, and many museums and churches have steps leading up to the entrance. In 2004 the city authorities announced a plan to install ramps on 80 of the bridges, but this has still not been implemented. So a companion is essential. There are several wheelchair lifts around the city which require a key, obtainable from the tourist office, Azienda di Promozione Turistica (APT), which has branches at the railway station, in the airport arrivals hall and near Piazza San Marco. From the railway station, a sloping path leads to the waterfront and the stop for the vaporetto No. 1, which zigzags along the Grand Canal. About two-thirds of the vaporetto lines are wheelchair-accessible. The best way of organizing your trip is to travel with a reliable company such as Accessible Italy, www.accessibleitaly.com; tel. +378-941111 or +378-0549-941111; fax +378-941110 or +378-0549-941110.

Driving
As Venice is traffic-free you will have to leave your vehicle in one of the multi-level car parks of Piazzale Roma, or on Tronchetto, terminal for the car ferry to the Lido, where driving is allowed.

Electricity
Except in the oldest areas of the city, the current is 220 V AC, 50 Hz. Take an adaptor for your appliances.

Emergencies
Police (carabinieri): ☎ 112
Emergency services: ☎ 113
First aid: ☎ 118
Ambulance: ☎ 041 523 00 00
Tourists in difficulty can call a help line by dialling 041 529 87 11.

Entry Regulations and Customs Allowance
If you are a citizen of an EU country, you can enter Italy with a National Identity Card; otherwise you will need a valid passport. Visas are required only for stays of more than 90 days.

Passengers aged 17 years and over, arriving with goods purchased duty-free in non-EU countries, may import 200 cigarettes or 50 cigars or 250 g tobacco; 1litre spirits over 22% or 2 litres dessert wine and sparkling wine;

2 litres table wine; 50 g perfume; 250 ml eau de toilette. Passengers from EU countries may import much larger quantities of goods, but duty-paid.

Finding Your Way

Venice is a small city and you can easily get around on foot. Signposted routes show the principal directions such as to Saint Mark's Square or the Rialto. However, as most addresses consist only of the name of the *sestiere* (district) and a number which can run into four figures, it is sometimes difficult to find an exact location. You can buy an *Indicatore anagrafico* which lists all the streets corresponding to the numbers.

It may be helpful to know the following terms. There is only one *piazza*, that of San Marco. The little square in front of each church is called a *campo*. These are sometimes bordered by canals, or they may be enclosed on three sides by dwellings, and many have a secluded, mysterious atmosphere. A *campiello* is similar, but smaller. A street is a *calle*, the narrower *calletta,* the cobbled *salizzada* or the dead-end *ramo*. A courtyard is *corte*, while *sottoportego* refers to a covered passageway. As for canals, wide ones are *canale*, smaller ones *rio*, and when filled-in, *rio terrà*. A quay is *riva*, or *fondamenta* when it's on the canalside, while a filled-in arm of the lagoon is the *piscina*.

Gondolas

The official rate is €75–80 for 6 passengers for 40 minutes, and €41 for every extra 25 minutes. The night tarif, valid 8pm–8am, is even higher. Settle the price with the gondolier before you climb aboard.

Official gondola landing stages *(imbarcadero)*:
Bacino Orseolo: ☎ 041 528 93 16
Danieli: Riva Schiavoni ☎ 041 522 22 54
Dogana: Calle Vallaresso ☎ 041 520 61 20
Ferrovia: S. Lucia ☎ 041 718 543
Piazzale Roma: ☎ 041 522 11 51
S. Maria del Giglio: ☎ 041 522 20 73
S. Marco: ☎ 041 520 06 85
S. Sofia: Pescheria, ☎ 041 522 28 44

S. Tomà: ☎ 041 520 52 75
Trinità: Campo S. Moisé, ☎ 041 523 18 37
Rialto: Riva Carbon, ☎ 041 522 49 04.

Lost Property

If you lose something on a vaporetto, go to the lost property office:
ACTV, St Angelo stop (No 9), ☎ 041 272 21 79
Other lost property is held in an office near the Rialto Bridge:
Ufficio all'Economato, Calle Loredan, Ca' Farsetti 4136

Post Office

If you want your mail to be delivered quickly, use the *Posta prioritaria* service, which works quite well (and put your postcards in an envelope).
Stamps *(francobolli)* are sold at post offices, in tobacconists and often in hotels. The main post office is on the Rialto, Mon–Sat 8.30am–6pm. 24-hour service for fax, express and registered post. Each district also has its post office, open in principle 8.30am–12.30 or 1.30pm. The San Marco post office is conveniently located opposite the Basilica.

Public Holidays

January 1	*Capodanno*	New Year's Day
January 6	*Befana*	Epiphany
April 25	*Festa di San Marco*	St Mark's Day
May 1	*Festa del Lavoro*	Labour Day
June 2	*Festa della Repubblica*	Republic Day
August 15	*Ferragosto*	Assumption
November 1	*Ognissanti*	All Saints' Day
December 8	*Immacolata Concezione*	Immaculate Conception
December 25	*Natale*	Christmas Day
December 26	*Santo Stefano*	St Stephen's Day
Moveable	*Lunedì di Pasqua*	Easter Monday

Local festivals:
February	Carnival
May	La Vogalonga: gondola race, Sunday after Ascension

3rd Sun July   Festa del Redentore
1st Sun Sept   Regata Storica: costumed regatta on the Grand Canal
November 21   Festa della Madonna della Salute

Public Transport

Vaporetto routes are frequently modified and it's better to consult the information posted at stops rather than rely on city maps which may be out of date. Several lines vary with the season. Line 1, the Accelerato, is in fact the slowest, providing a magnificent cruise on the Grand Canal at little cost.

The *motoscafo* resembles the vaporetto but makes fewer stops.

The *motonave* serve longer routes, to the Lido for example. *Motonave* tie up at Stazione Marittima and Riva degli Schiavoni.

Traghetto are ferries, which cross the Grand Canal at seven different points. Green signs indicate the stops.

For information call at the ACTV offices, Calle dei Fuseri, Palazzo Regina Vittoria, open Mon–Fri 8.30am–6pm; Sat 8.30am–1pm, or Piazzale Roma, open daily 7.30am–8pm.

Tickets. On the Canal Grande a one-way ticket, valid 60 minutes, costs €5. A day ticket (€12) is valid on all the lines. You can buy a 3-day pass for €25, which includes the transport of one piece of hand luggage.

The Tourist Office issues a special card, Rolling Venice, for young people between 14 and 29 which entitles them to various discounts including a "72 hours" travel pass which is obtainable for €15 at the Piazzale Roma office. Holders must carry another means of identification with a photograph. (Prices as of summer 2006).

Religious Services

Mass is celebrated in Italian in all the Catholic churches and also in Latin in Saint Mark's at 10am on Sundays. To hear Gregorian chant, go to Sunday Mass at 11am at the church of San Giorgio Maggiore.

Sightseeing Passes

The Museum Pass, €18, grants entrance to the museums of St Mark's Square, the museums of 18th-century culture (Ca' Rezzonico, Palazzo

Mocenigo and Casa Goldoni), and the Island museums (Murano Glass and Burano Lace). It is valid for three months and covers single entry to each museum. Reductions are available for children aged 6 to 14, students aged 15 to 29 and EU citizens over 65. Free entry to children up to 5, and disabled people with escort.

The Venice Card exists in two versions, Orange and Blue, for 1, 3 or 7 days. The Orange card gives free access to public transport, toilet-nurseries, municipal museums, reductions for many exhibitions and cultural events, in car parks and bars, restaurants and shops, among other benefits. The Blue card is similar but gives reductions rather than free entry to the mueums. Cards can be reserved up to 48 hours before your arrival on www.venicecard.com, or phone the Call Center (+39 041 2424) daily 8am–7.30pm. You will be given a reservation number and details of the pick-up point where you can collect your card.

The Chorus pass, €8, gives access to 15 historic churches. Proceeds go towards maintaining and restoring the city's artistic heritage. Single tickets €2.50. On sale in the churches, Venice Pavillion and at travel agencies. ☎ 041 2750462, fax 041 2750 494 or see www.chorusvenezia.org

Taxis

The *taxi acquei* or *motoscafi di nolo* (water taxis) wait at a dozen stations. The prices are fixed, but it's always better to come to an agreement with the driver before you set off. From the airport to the centre estimate €90; Piazzale Roma to the centre €80. There is also the possibility of an hourly rate, €75. In the historic centre, the rate is fixed at €15.49 for the first seven minutes, then €0.25 for every following 15 seconds. But there are numerous extras for luggage, night service, holidays, etc. (Prices as of summer 2006.)
Central telephone (24-hour service): 041 240 67 12

Telephone

Public phones function with phonecards, sold at post offices, bars, tobacconists, some newspaper kiosks, the headquarters for Italian telecommunications and the station. Before you use a card for the first time, tear off the corner.

In a public telephone centre you pay at the counter after the call is completed. These centres are next to the post office near the Rialto, at Ruga Vecchia San Giovanni, at Santa Lucia Station and at the telecommunications office on Piazzale Roma.

The outgoing international code is 00. Then dial the country code (UK 44; USA and Canada 1) and the area code without the initial zero, followed by the local number.

For local calls you have to dial the entire number including the initial 0.

For enquiries, dial 1240.

Tides

For information on the tides (and to know if you need to go out in your wellies) ☎ 041 241 19 96. The *acqua alta* (high water) makes its annual incursion into the city every winter, when the municipality lays out stacks of sturdy benches to form boardwalks along strategic streets.

Tipping

Service charges are included in restaurants, but you can leave a few extra coins. It is usual to tip the hotel porter, the doorman or anyone else who does you a small service.

Tourist Offices

At the offices of the *Azienda d Promozione Turistica* (ATP) you can pick up useful free brochures and maps. *Un Ospite di Venezia*, available in hotels, is full of information on what's on. The offices are at:

Piazza San Marco 71F, ☎ 041 529 87 11

Palazzetto della Selva, Giardinetti Reali, San Marco, ☎ 041 522 51 50

Stazione Santa Lucia, ☎ 041 529 87 11

Piazzale Roma – Garage ASM, ☎ 041 529 87 11

A useful number for tourists is 800 355 920, Venezia No Problem, where you can lodge complaints about poor service.

Water

Tap water is safe to drink, and there are drinking fountains all over the city. Water unfit for drinking it is marked with a sign: *Acqua non potabile*.

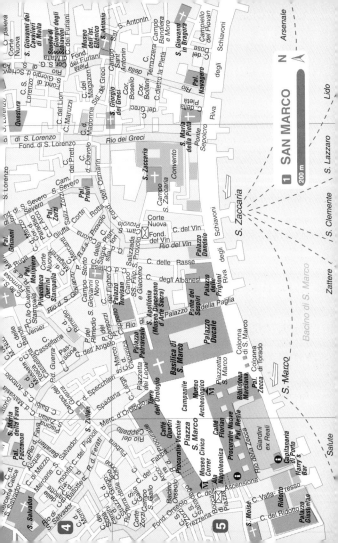

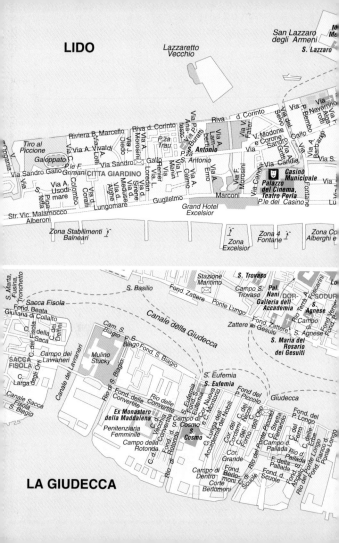

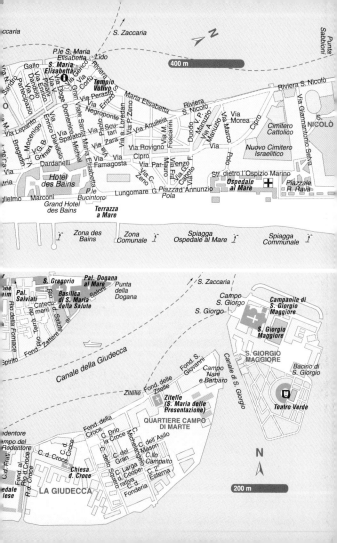

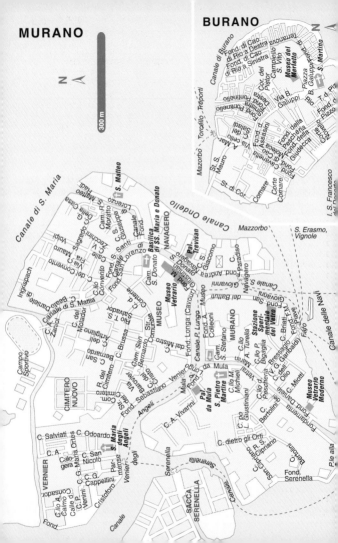

Ala Napoleonica 28
Antico Cimitero Israelitico 72
Arco del Paradiso 68
Arsenale 67
Ateneo Veneto 28
Bacari 79
Basilica di San Marco 20–21
– di Santa Maria della
  Salute 33, 35, 40
– dei Santi Maria e Donato
  73–74
Biblioteca Nazionale
  Marciana 23
Biennale Internazionale
  d'Arte 67
Burano 74, 82
Ca' Corner della Regina 31
Ca' Farsetti 32
Ca' Foscari 32
Ca' Loredan 32
Ca' d'Oro 31, 61
Ca' Pesaro 31, 42, 44
Ca' Rezzonico 32, 38
Ca' Venier dei Leoni 32
Ca' Zane 44
Campanile di San Marco 22
Campiello Mosca 39
Campo delle Beccarie 53
– Ghetto Novo 62
– delle Gorne 67
– della Maddalena 60
– della Pescheria 53
– San Geremia 62
– San Giacomo dell'Orio 44
– San Maurizio 28
– San Polo 54
– San Stefano 28
– San Tomà 54
– San Zan Degola 44
– Sant'Alvise 62
– Santa Maria Formosa 68
– Santa Margherita 38
Carnival 51, 57
Casa Goldoni 52, 54

Casino 87
Cattedrale di Santa Maria
  Assunta 75
Chiostro di Sant'Apollonia
  68
Collezione Peggy
  Guggenheim 35, 40
– Vittorio Cini 35
Corte del Million 61
Dogana da Mar 33
Erberia 53
Fabbriche Nuove 31
– Vecchie 31
Florian 78
Fondaco dei Tedeschi 31
– dei Turchi 31, 44
Fondamenta Nuove 61
– della Sensa 60
– Venier-Savorgnan 58–59
Fondazione Querini-
  Stampalia 65
Frezzeria 28
Galleria d'Arte Moderna 42
– Franchetti 34
Gallerie dell'Accademia
  32, 34
Gesuiti 61
Giardini Pubblici 67
Ghetto 62
Gondolas 33, 56
Gran Teatro La Fenice
  25, 87
Grand Canal 30–33
Harry's Bar 86
I Gesuati 36, 40
Il Redentore 70
International Film
  Festival 89
La Giudecca 70, 82
Lido 71–72, 82
Madonna dell'Orto 60
Mercatino
  Antiquariato 25
Murano 72–74, 82

Museo Archeologico 23
– d'Arte Orientale 42
– Civico Correr 22
– Civico di Storia
  Naturale 43
– Comunità Ebraica 60, 62
– del Merletto 74
– Diocesano d'Arte
  Sacra 68
– Storico Navale 67
– del Vetro 73
Palazzi Mocenigo 32
Palazzo Albrizzi 52
– Balbi 32
– Bellavite 28
– Bembo 32
– Contarini delle Figure 32
– Corner 32, 54
– Da Ponte 28
– Dario 32, 40
– Dolfin Manin 31
– Ducale 24
– Grassi 25, 32
– Grimani 32
– Gritti 28
– Labia 62
– Loredan-Mocenigo 28
– della Madonnetta 32
– Maffetti-Tiepolo 54
– Mocenigo 44
– Molin 28
– Papadopoli 32
– Priuli 62, 68
– Querini-Stampalia 68
– Salvadego 28
– Soranzo 34
– Surian-Bellotto 62
– Vendramin-Calergi 30
– Zaguri 28
– Zane-Collalto 54
– Zorzi 68
Parco Savorgnan 62
Pescheria 31
Piazza San Marco 33

Pietà 66
Ponte dell'Accademia 25, 28, 32
– delle Guglie 58, 62
– dei Pugni 38
– di Rialto 24–25
– degli Scalzi 43
– dei Sospiri 24
– delle Tette 52
– dei Tre Archi 62
Quartiere Saffa 62
Painting 46–49
Punta della Dogana 40
Rialto markets 52–53
Rio de San Trovaso 36–37
Riva di Biasio 44
– degli Schiavoni 66
Sala Concerti del Circolo Artistico 65
Salizzada San Lio 65, 68
San Fantin 28
San Francesco della Vigna 67
San Giacomo dell'Orio 43
San Giacomo di Rialto 53
San Giobbe 59, 62
San Giorgio dei Greci 66
San Giorgio Maggiore 70–71
San Giovanni in Bràgora 66
San Giovanni Crisostomo 61
San Lazzaro degli Armeni 71
San Lio 68
San Marcuola 59
San Martino 74
San Moisè 25, 28
San Nicolò (Lido) 72
San Nicolò dei Mendicoli 37
San Nicolò da Tolentino 43–44
San Pantalon 38–39
San Pietro Martire 74
San Polo 52, 54
San Rocco 50
San Salvador 24
San Samuele 32

San Sebastiano 37, 40
San Simeone Piccolo 30
San Stae 31, 43, 44
San Vidal 28
Sant'Alvise 60
Santa Fosca 75
Santa Maria del Carmelo 38
Santa Maria del Giglio 28
Santa Maria Formosa 65, 68
Santa Maria Gloriosa dei Frari 51, 54
Santa Maria Mater Domini 42–43, 44
Santa Maria dei Miracoli 64
Santa Maria della Misericordia 60
Santa Maria di Nazareth degli Scalzi 30, 58, 62
Sant'Angelo Raffaele 37
Sant'Eufemia 70
Santi Giovanni e Paolo 64–65
Santo Stefano 25
Scala Contarini del Bòvolo 25
Scuola di San Giorgio degli Schiavoni 67
– Grande dei Carmini 37–38
– Grande di San Giovanni Evangelista 50–51, 54
– Grande di San Rocco 50, 54
Shopping 26–27, 54
Squero San Trovaso 40
Teatro Fondamenta Nuove 87
– Goldoni 87
– Malibran 87
– Toniolo 87
Torcello 75, 82
Torre dell'Orologio 23
Zattere 35–36, 40

GENERAL EDITOR
Barbara Ender
FEATURES AND WALKS
Jack Altman
RESEARCH
Francesca Grazzi
and Edris Rahimi
COVER DESIGN
Jérôme Curchod
www.thebonusroom.com
PHOTO CREDITS
Guy Minder, except:
R. Holzbachová/P. Bénet:
pp. 8, 12, 30 (r), 39, 51, 86
Wysocki/hemis.fr: pp. 14, 33
Boisvieux/hemis.fr: p. 74
Barbara Ender: p. 83
MAPS
Elsner & Schichor;
JPM Publications

Copyright © 2006, 1994
by JPM Publications S.A.
12, avenue William-Fraisse,
1006 Lausanne, Switzerland
information@jpmguides.com
http://www.jpmguides.com/

Printed in Switzerland
Weber/Bienne (CTP)
11101.00.0142
Edition 2006–2007